Thunderbolts over Burma

The 34 Squadron standard with the 'Burma 1944-1945' battle honour. (*Courtesy of Andrew Thomas*)

Thunderbolts over Burma

A Pilot's War Against the Japanese in 1945 and the Battle of Sittang Bend

Angus Findon with Mark Hillier

AIR WORLD

First published in Great Britain in 2020 by
Air World Books
An imprint of
Pen & Sword Books Ltd
Yorkshire – Philadelphia

Copyright © Angus Findon with Mark Hillier 2020

ISBN 978 1 52677 966 3

The right of Angus Findon with Mark Hillier to be identified as Authors of this work has been asserted by them in accordance with the Copyright, Designs and Patents Act 1988.

A CIP catalogue record for this book is
available from the British Library.

All rights reserved. No part of this book may be reproduced or transmitted in any form or by any means, electronic or mechanical including photocopying, recording or by any information storage and retrieval system, without permission from the Publisher in writing.

Typeset by Mac Style
Printed and bound in the UK by TJ International Ltd,
Padstow, Cornwall.

Pen & Sword Books Limited incorporates the imprints of Atlas, Archaeology, Aviation, Discovery, Family History, Fiction, History, Maritime, Military, Military Classics, Politics, Select, Transport, True Crime, Air World, Frontline Publishing, Leo Cooper, Remember When, Seaforth Publishing, The Praetorian Press, Wharncliffe Local History, Wharncliffe Transport, Wharncliffe True Crime and White Owl.

For a complete list of Pen & Sword titles please contact

PEN & SWORD BOOKS LIMITED
47 Church Street, Barnsley, South Yorkshire, S70 2AS, England
E-mail: enquiries@pen-and-sword.co.uk
Website: www.pen-and-sword.co.uk

Or

PEN AND SWORD BOOKS
1950 Lawrence Rd, Havertown, PA 19083, USA
E-mail: Uspen-and-sword@casematepublishers.com
Website: www.penandswordbooks.com

Contents

Foreword vi

Introduction x

Acknowledgements xxiv

Chapter 1 King and Country 1

Chapter 2 L.A.C. Findon, Pilot 19

Chapter 3 Burma 36

Chapter 4 Operation *Birdcage* 66

Chapter 5 Spitfire! 82

Chapter 6 Last Days 90

Appendix I: Summary of Events, June to September 1945 96

Appendix II: Record of Events Relating to Angus Findon's Sorties, July to August 1945 111

Appendix III: The Battle of the Sittang Bend 118

Appendix IV: Operations Birdcage *and* Mastiff*: The Liberation of Allied Prisoners of War and Internees* 123

Appendix V: Reproduction of pages from Angus Findon's Pilot's Logbook 127

Foreword

It was 3 August 1987, and the setting was Neill Anderson's second-hand bookshop in Nightingale Court, Blandford, Dorset. I drove over to have my once-weekly coffee with Neill and check his modest stock under the headboard of *The Second Reading Bookshop*. Neill, being fairly new to dealing but learning fast, valued my advice on prices and scarcity, in those days well before today's internet. Being a 'professional' book collector of many years, I was able to advise him as well as discover titles I fancied for myself.

One such was the logbook of RAF pilot Angus Findon. I was surprised, as at the time these things were uncommon on the open market. Handing it to me, Neill said, 'Came in yesterday. The chap wanted £50 for it. I'll put it in at £70. Do you think that's fair? It can be £60 to you.' I was even more surprised to see that not only was the log complete, including all his Second World War flying service, with the mandatory pages initialled by his squadron leader CO to boot, but it was also illustrated with various ephemera including active service photos tipped in.

'Was it his log?' I asked.

'Yes. Seems so,' replied Neill.

'How unusual,' I said. 'Wartime pilots were allowed to keep their logbooks and they treasure them close to their chests. They only appear for sale after they die. Neill, these things fetch around £120 now, but this one is very unusual. It really should go to auction and let it find its level, as I don't know what it's really worth. Of course, I would like it for myself but what would you say if I paid you the £60 but hand it back, gratis, to the vendor? After all, we both owe our existence to wartime fliers like him and, I don't know if you agree, but he must surely feel a pang of dismay in having to part with it? So, I'd like to give it back to him with a note from us both saying why. But why on earth did he want to get rid of it?'

'A bit short of the readies, apparently,' Neill said.

'All the more reason we should return it to him,' I replied.

'Meanwhile, at least he will know it is safe and not gone for good.

Should he ever want to ease his conscience and reimburse me when times are easier, of course that would be fine. By the way, have you his address?'

'Lives not far away,' Niell said. 'Barnside at Rixon, Sturminster Newton, on the way into the town from Shaftesbury.'

So, after perusing it for a couple of days and impressed by its contents (he flew more than 14 types of aircraft) I wrote Angus Findon a little note and asked if I could bring it over – not wanting any money for it – which I hoped he would accept as an appreciation of his wartime service. It did seem pretty hairy, especially against the Japanese. I got a phone call saying how grateful, and not a little embarrassed, he was for such a kind gesture, suggesting we meet at 'The Rose' café in Sturminster. In the end he asked me to keep the logbook for him strictly under wraps until after his death. I have it still. When I go, it is safely bequeathed to the author of this book.

The date of our meeting was Thursday, 20 August 1987. I arrived at the café early, as I usually do with appointments, and heard a very loud motorbike (it turned out to be a rare German antique) pull up outside in a cloud of blue smoke. A large figure in the doorway divested itself of what I assumed was a huge, all-enveloping flying-jacket, goggles, helmet and gauntlets.

'I'm Angus,' he said, proffering a hand. Such was my introduction to this eccentric character. Mid-sixties, wearing his years well, clean-shaven and spruce, with a cultured, well-modulated voice. After describing his present circumstances in retirement on a rather meagre RAF pension and despite the tendency to dive down conversational rabbit holes, ('Yes, you were saying – what happened next?') I took to him at once.

Married, rather lonely I guessed, he started on a most interesting, even captivating history of his flying training, then especially of his war years, with some of his anecdotes being quite extraordinary and, to me, ringing true. For all of three hours I was quite enthralled and at times astonished by what he told me of things which went on behind the scenes of the RAF at the end of the Second World War.

'Angus,' I said, 'all this is fascinating and historically, even socio-historically, important. Have you written any of it down? If not, I'm a writer and need to get down as much of what you have told me this afternoon – for your approval of course.'

Vehemently, he replied, 'No way! Some of what happened could be actionable if it gets out. People concerned are still alive. Keep it to yourself!'

'I'll tell you what I'll do,' he went on, 'I'll record a narrative on tape for you to keep until I'm gone. I'm quite good at recording and have some taped material done from the time. Then, once I'm out of it, let's tell the world, sounds and all.'

Angus was as good as his word. Several weeks later, he delivered two sets of tapes in fragile mini-cassettes which, not having the proper gear, I played on the car radio. They were absolutely amazing. His clear, well-spoken narrative was embellished by the sound of Spits and T-bolts (Spitfire 8s and P-47 Thunderbolts. The latter was easily his favourite fighter) revving up before sorties and taking off. I had them transferred to the sturdier CD disks which the author of this book now has.

Over two years, we got to know each other well, Angus giving me various wartime items such as silk escape-maps, documents, squadron orders, his paybooks and a Japanese army dagger which, when nailed up on a post as a decoy, was used to direct Japanese troops into their own minefields. Copies of two of his three books, too. He even offered me his wartime medals which of course I firmly refused: they really are family heirlooms.

Building a new, self-employed career after 30 years of working for others, I have been too busy working in thirty-three countries to create the book which Angus so rightly deserves, and am delighted that Mark Hillier has taken on the task which you are certain to find so engrossing.

John Gadd

John Gadd, an international consultant in cost-effective pig production, is well-known for his lifetime illustrated diary of some 5 million words and 36,000 illustrations in 160 volumes, which the Dorset History Centre has accepted in perpetuity. He published his 3,000th article on pigs in December 2018, following a major textbook for the Chinese pig industry which has sold 8,000 copies in its first year – thought to be a record for an agricultural textbook.

Introduction

Fortunately for those of us interested in air operations of the Second World War, many first-hand accounts exist in the form of autobiographies, histories and some sound recordings.

As time marches on, however, the chances of unearthing new stories are diminishing all too rapidly, as are the survivors of those heady, exhilarating but dangerous days when the world tore itself apart.

Very occasionally, however, we are lucky to happen across a story that has not been told and one such rare example is that of Angus Findon, presented here.

By chance, I was having a conversation with an ex-airline pilot friend and fellow aviation enthusiast about risk in aviation and we got around to talking about air operations in the Far East in the Second World War. He mentioned he had been listening to a sound recording made by a Sussex man who flew the P-47 for the RAF in Burma. He said it was a fascinating tale of his training, conversion to the P-47 and finally operations in the last few months of the war in the Far East.

I was lucky enough to be able to borrow the disks and spent hours listening to the voice of a man I had never met but who blew me away with his story-telling. I loved his ability to bring to life his trials and tribulations and the risks involved in aviation.

So detailed and exhilarating were his accounts, I was instantly hooked. The manner in which he conveyed both his fear and, at the same time, his anxiety as he started the powerful 2800 horsepower, 18-cylinder, radial engine of a P-47 thunderbolt, when he was about to head out on his first operational sortie, was riveting.

In addition to his period of combat, he enriched his story with details of his training, the characters he met and the lead up to the culminating moment when he qualified as a combat-ready pilot. The result is an absorbing story about an infrequently-described aircraft in a theatre of operations given comparatively little attention.

Angus joined 34 Squadron in June 1945, towards the end of the war, after many months of trying to join an operational unit. This squadron was formed during 1916 and served as an Army Co-operation unit, both on the Western Front and later on the Italian Front, but on return to the UK, it was disbanded at RAF Old Sarum in 1919. Reforming in December 1935, it started life as a Blenheim squadron based in Singapore where the squadron was virtually decimated. It was reformed in India in August 1942, with Blenheim IVs, after the Japanese had entered the war. In April 1943, 34 Squadron converted to a fighter – bomber squadron, operating over Burma from November 1943, with the Hurricane IIc. It continued in this role until the end of the war, converting to the Republic Thunderbolt in March 1945, by which time they had advanced deep into Burma. 34 Squadron was disbanded on 15 October 1945.

When Angus arrived with a small band of pilots, who had already been trained on the Thunderbolt, the squadron was in the process of converting to the Thunderbolt II from the trusty Hurricane IIC at Kwetnge, in the Mandalay Region of what is today Myanmar.

P-47s were operated by several Allied air arms during the Second World War, including the RAF which initially ordered 240 razorback P-47Ds which they designated 'Thunderbolt Mark I'. Subsequently the RAF ordered 590 P-47 D-25s which had a Pratt and Whitney R-2800-59 Double Wasp 18 Cylinder engine and a bubble canopy. The fuel capacity was also increased from 305 to 370 gallons. This became known as the 'Thunderbolt Mark II'. It was this aircraft that started to replace the RAF's ageing Hurricanes IIBs in Asia for ground-attack purposes.

With no need for another high-altitude fighter, the RAF adapted their Thunderbolts for ground attack, a task for which the type was well suited. Once the Thunderbolts were cleared for use in 1944, they were used against the Japanese in Burma by sixteen RAF squadrons of the South East Asia Command from India. Operations with Army support (operating as 'cab ranks' to be called in when needed) consisted of attacks on enemy airfields and lines of communication and escort sorties. They proved devastating, in tandem with Spitfires, during the Japanese breakout attempt at the Sittang Bend in the final months of the war. The Thunderbolts were armed with three 500 lb (227 kg) bombs or, in some cases, '60 pound' RP-3 rocket projectiles. Long-range fuel tanks could be fitted and gave up to five hours of endurance.

Angus had been fortunate to gain experience of the type at an operational training unit but some pilots had to find out about their new aircraft in theatre, often with precious little training. One other pilot who converted to the Thunderbolt in Burma was the commanding officer of 258 Squadron, Squadron Leader Neil Cameron (later to become Marshal of the Royal Air Force) who found the aircraft a joy to fly but thought it needed respect which one of his pilots ignored:

> Our first aircraft arrived on the 8 September [1944] and with them two American instructors who had a lot of experience on the aircraft. What a delight it was to have brand new aircraft and a type which we knew the Japanese would respect. As it was a single seat aircraft, my pilots could only have a comprehensive ground briefing before being showing them the cockpit and being sent on their first solo. It was all manged with the minimum incident.
>
> The Thunderbolt was proving an excellent ground-attack aircraft as well as a pure fighter and long range escorter of bombers. It was heavy and, once put into a dive, few aircraft could stay with it. The Japanese fighters of the day were light and very manoeuvrable and could easily turn inside the Spitfire or Hurricane. But the Thunderbolt could dive away or use the extra speed to climb out of range.[1]

The speed was a tactical advantage, for sure, but for some the temptation to go fast became too much:

> One problem was that the aircraft was heavy and fast and had a powerful engine. One of my more adventurous Australian pilots thought he would try to dive it with full throttle and see how fast it would actually go. He should have known better, and he spread the aircraft and himself over the Southern most states of India …

---

1. Marshal of the Royal Air Force Lord Cameron of Balhousie, *In the Midst of Things* (Hodder and Stoughton, London, 1985), p.82.

This was the first experience many of us had with the sound barrier, or Mach 1 as it came to be known. The word then was compressibility. It meant the same thing, but aviators were just beginning to learn about he problem ahead of them.[2]

Angus writes about his experiences with this new phenomenon and he too witnessed a number of crashes that occurred due to pilots not fully understanding the aerodynamics at play during a high-speed dive in the Thunderbolt which, due to its weight, accelerated very quickly. Many paid the ultimate price while getting used to their new steeds.

By the time Angus arrived on 34 Squadron, the conversion process was underway and the squadron summary of operations for the period certainly makes interesting reading. It's clear that the new aircraft was, initially, only cautiously welcomed after having fought to date in their trusty Hawker Hurricanes:

During April, May and June a slightly chaotic state was caused by weather, change of location and conversion from Hurricanes to Thunderbolts. That does not sound at all impressive – in fact the bare details are definitely dull – but behind those dry particulars, and I don't mean the weather, the stage was being set for something new. In July, the players knew their parts ; they were equipped for a public appearance and shortly the Japs would be aware of a show that was going to be a big hit. I refer of course to the conversion, the new era of 34 Squadron who had operated against the Japs on Blenheims and Hurries from the days of Singapore.

A pilot likes his aircraft; to him it is the prefect aircraft and one does not change one's battle office with as little concern as changing a pair of trousers. The Hurricane was the figurehead of innumerable tales of aerial success and traditions, but the Thunderbolt came as a stranger. Different habits and an accent as unlike the hum of a Merlin as the two Nations who use it.

The P-47 was designed as a high-level patrol fighter and an escort for the Fortress and Liberators of the U.S Bombardment Group.

---

2. Lord Cameron of Balhousie, p.81.

With its turbo supercharger, it is eminently suited to such duties, but near the ground it is rather like making a fat swimmer race in treacle. No-one will deny it is operating in a secondary capacity, but I challenge anyone to say it's not achieving first rate results.

The pilots accepted this newcomer without prejudice, and it has not let them down. Nine members [including Angus Findon] were direct from O.T.U where they had chosen Thunderbolt in preference to the Spitfire. Their reasons were sound. A radial engine is immune from the problems confronting a liquid cooled motor in hot climates and, with its long range, it could make the most of the weather where monsoon conditions often hampered operations.

As the USAAF had shown during the fight in Europe, where almost all single-engine aircraft had come down to low level activity, it was a useful weapon for bombing and strafing. Jokes were made by the fellows training on Spits. 'Evasion action in the T' Bolt is taken by undoing your straps and running round the cockpit,' they used to say. But the chaps were confident and keen about operating in the Flying Battleship.

Those of the pilots who had converted were quick to appreciate its qualities and the Wolf pack showed its fangs. Operating from Meiktela [July to August 1945] a bomb load as heavy as possible, and 34, proud of its close support to the Army were ready to take on any target and blast the Japs to the land of their ancestors.

No finer opportunity could be desired than the mass attempt of the enemy to escape during July. Targets were good and on the nursery slopes of the Pegu Yomas and the Sittang valley, where the opposition was slight, the pilots learnt how to lay their bombs bang on the target and brought their standard of air-to-ground firing up to such a pitch of perfection that each pilot knew when a tightening of the finger would send a rush of .5 into a foxhole of suspicious looking basha. When the time comes for the next campaign, 34 will look forward to as much action as they can get and, if we are fortunate enough to be in at the kill when Singapore is deloused, we shall feel thoroughly happy to fly in the same skies as the Blenheims who first formed our squadron.'

Angus started on operations out of Meiktela in July of 1945 at about the time of the Battle of the Sittang Bend and the Japanese breakout across Pegu Yomas between 2 July and 7 August 1945. These were linked Japanese military operations during the Burma Campaign which took place nearly at the end of the Second World War.

Surviving elements of the Japanese Army, who had been driven into the Pegu Yoma, attempted to break out eastwards to join other Japanese troops retreating from the British forces. The breakout was the objective of the Japanese Twenty-Eighth Army with support, at first, from the Thirty-Third Army and later the Fifteenth Army. The start of this phase was signified by the Japanese Thirty-Third Army attacking Allied positions in the Sittang Bend, near the mouth of the river, to distract the Allies.

The British had been alerted to the break-out attempt and it ended in disaster for the Japanese, who suffered many losses, with some formations being completely wiped out.

Around 14,000 Japanese were lost, with well over half being killed, while British forces suffered only 95 killed and 322 wounded. The breakout attempt and the ensuing battle became the last significant land battle of the Allied armies in the Second World War.

Angus with 34 along with 42 Squadron, equipped with Thunderbolts, plus 607 and 273 Squadrons equipped with the Mk VIII Spitfire, were all in the mix giving air support through the use of visual control posts. This meant the troops on the ground had excellent air support and, despite often poor weather conditions, the RAF kept up the pressure on the Japanese. This extract, from the Squadron Operational Record Book, (ORB) best describes the squadron's role in the July and August period of 1945:

> The following is a general outline of the situation of Military Operations which go hand-in-hand with the work done by this Squadron in July, and which is considered to be the last phase in the Burma conflict.
>
> Split by the rapid thrust our armies made from Manadaly to Rangoon, the Japs lost any strategic advantage they may have held. Left to them were the tactics of escape. While victory parades were taking place in Rangoon, many thousands of Japs lay up in the Pegu

Yomas and others fought a rear-guard action along such routes as the Mawchi road. Obviously, this isolated Jap army would need supplies and more plain was the fact that they could not get them. Came July and they were massed for a break through. From Toungoo south, they started to filter across heading for the Sittang where it was 'Cross or Die'. Weakened by disease and shortage of food they were given four pieces of bamboo with which to float themselves across the river. They had a few handfuls of rice and a small amount of ammunition. Pretty desperate measures.

From Mokpalin, East of the Sittang, they attempted to form a bridge head and, spreading out in the swampy paddy, they tried to push a wedge into our lines to help their retreating forces making for a temporary respite in the Moulmein areas. Deprived of mountain cover and the low cloud which kept them covered and safe from the air, they stepped into the valley and slaughter commenced. By the end of the first week they knew it would cost them but they continued. They had to.

Not all sorties to aid targets identified by the army were successful due to the often-appalling weather, and Angus Findon found himself on one such sortie on the 9 July 1945 which the Squadron ORB relates:

Abortive operations are bound to occur, but what was not shown on the sortie report or known to anyone but the pilots concerned, is the degree of effort which was made before the monsoon won the argument. Here is an example of such an operation. Two flights took off early in an attempt to reach, respectively, the lower Sittang area and an enemy troop concentration west of Toungoo. If those going to the Sittang area were held up by the weather, they would return and attack the target assigned to the second flight in the foothills. For quite a distance, the forward flight could be seen spread out some three miles away, small black dots against the sky. Over the R/T we could hear them commenting on the cloud as they passed information back to us. They were going through a gap and suggested we might try the same way. Closing the formation, we wriggled through and stooged along between the layers. At this stage one of the No. 2s in the first flight fell too far behind his No. 1 and became separated from the formation. It cost him his life. As was his duty, the No. 1 remained to try and contact the missing pilot. The other three got through and bombed the target. Dash and discretion are wisely tempered but no pilot of 34 who realises his obligation to the Army – and all of them do – will be satisfied unless he knows it was absolutely impossible to penetrate the weather. The ground crews take pride in their squadron when it comes back without its bombs and the other Squadrons, on the same day, return with loaded racks 'Push on regardless'.[3]

Angus was up again on the 17 July in Thunderbolt KL201 for a two-hour army-support operation to attack the Mawchi road with bombs and several staffing runs:

The road to Mawchi is a difficult one for the Army. Low cloud prevents regular air support, the roads impede transport and Jap lingers in the jungle. To displace him is not easy. However, there were times, such as the 17th of July, when 34 were able to put a flight over the mountains. The brown jobs were being held up by Jap cross fire where the muddy road straightened to cross a chaung. The bomb line was 400 yards from our target and mortar smoke showed us where the enemy were. Bombs tore gaps in the jungle and strafing runs sprayed the dense cover. We hope it helped the army.[4]

The entry in the Squadron Operations Record Book gives some further information on this Army support operation and this time the weather remained favourable for the sortie:

Japanese positions on a bend in the Mawchi road at QB204939, were holding up our own troops who were compelled to cross open ground and a chaung. Weather in the target area was excellent and smoke laid by artillery indicated the enemy's position. Dense jungle prevented the observation of any details but the bombs all fell in the

---

3. The National Archives (TNA), AIR 27/376. For a transcription of the Summary of Events for June to September 1945, see Appendix I.
4. TNA, AIR 27/376.

spot marked causing good explosions, one of which was followed by thick, grey smoke. The Jungle was well sprayed in six strafing runs…

One afternoon, 34 squadron were at readiness and frequent showers made a job seem unlikely. Some thought that it was a joke when the A.L.O [Army Liaison Officer] told them to report for immediate briefing. The strip was considered U/S. But the breakthrough had started with a rush and the Army had targets for us. A message was sent to the Group Captain for his decision to take off on the soaking strip and, by the time briefing was over, permission had been granted. A terrific atmosphere had been built up in a few minutes. It would be a gamble but, had they not taken to the air, disappointment would have been great. The chaps boarded their transport and went off yelling the familiar slogan of 34, 'Push on regardless.' The scramble was complete and the form-up was an achievement in itself. Low cloud and local storms made the task of seeing aircraft ahead a tricky business, but they did it and the next flight, as they started their engines, saw them disappear into the one blue gap which threw open the course for Pyu.[5]

Angus Findon was on his fifth operational sortie with the squadron when this flap started on the 21 July 1945. By then his regular mount was Thunderbolt II KL201 and he took off with his flight at 15.05 hours for the target area, landing at 18.15 hours – a sortie time of three hours.

What had happened was that on the 21 July the Japanese began the last and most desperate attempt to cross the Sittang river with the remaining 15,000 troops, many of whom were sick, in a last-ditch effort. The 54th Division, having suffered heavily from cholera and dysentery, came down from the Pegu Yomas mountain range and crossed the flooded paddy fields to the Sittang river. This led to maximum effort, and all available resources – tanks, guns, mortar and machine-gun, including air support – were immediately thrown in against them and, despite the the clouds and heavy rains, 34 Squadron were in the thick of the action.

---

5. TNA, AIR 27/376.

The Operations Record Book continues:

> They arrived to receive instructions from V.C.P Chico [visual control post] who was throwing out targets like jam tarts on a Sunday School outing and the air was full of various callsigns, map references and once or twice the sound of machine-gun fire as a pilot spoke to his section as he strafed. 34 took on a village and left it in ruins. As they set course for base, other flights of Spits and T Bolts could be seen belting down on targets. One aircraft alone killed 150 Japs out of a group sighted in open ground.
>
> Weather had closed in North of Toungoo and the pilots stayed there the night. From the strip, 37s were pounding the enemy 8 miles away and one could feel the atmosphere of war which at Meiktila seemed so far away. Throughout the night, small parties of Japs were prowling around the town, presumably raiding to obtain food, and spasmodic bursts of gunfire and the explosion of grenades continues till early morning.

The Operational Record Book records the sortie in brief with an entry about being in 'cabrank order' which was basically a system developed to provide close support for the Army, using the 'cab rank' system, with aircraft circling over the battlefield waiting for instructions from controllers travelling with the troops:

> In cabrank order, the first flight arrived to be directed to VCP Chico. Given the village of TAGUNGAING, QA94341, the a/c laid their bombs in positions which thoroughly wrecked the village and then went in to strafe it twice. Weather closed in toward base and the flight returned to land at TOUNGOO. Brake failure caused one aircraft to leave the runway and it sustained slight damage in a nose-over on soft ground. The pilot was unhurt.

Angus was flying pretty much every day for the rest of July with attacks on troop concentrations, strafing and bombing boats on rivers, attacking villages and bashas. One sortie of the 24 July is typical, and the Operational Record Book gives an account of the mission with Angus flying his trusty KL201 for a sortie time of 2.30 hours:

Japanese concentrations in the West half of Wegyi, from QB014495 to 010489, were bombed and strafed. 'A' Flight arrived punctually on target and smoke indication was given as first aircraft commenced bombing dive. Pilots were instructed to precision bomb various sectors and the desired results were achieved. Four bombs failed to explode but the remainder caused sufficient destruction to make up for this. The following four strafing runs are known to have affected the majority of the bashas but unfortunately no fires were caused due to the dampness. 'B' Flight closely followed the last attack and placed their 12 bombs along the line of bashas though these were considerably depleted by the results of 'A' Flight's attacks. Two strafing runs were made but it was impossible to see much on account of the trees.

On the 28th of the month the squadron was again called into action at 12.30 hours with six aircraft of 'A' flight taking off, heavily laden in the heat of the mid-day sun and humidity for a tiring three hours sortie, Angus again flying his regular mount KL201:

Jap troops were reported to be dug in at KYAUKSAUNG. Suspected positions were to be strafed on the bund and the south bank of the river extending to LETPADAN. Twelve miles east of PYU and the target was seen as a long, narrow village with many bashas. The greatest concentration of these was at the west end and this was the target for 12 bombs. Two bombs failed to explode but 6 which fell among the basahs caused heavy damage and 4 direct hits. As the Leader pulled out from his bombing attack, he noticed 6 or 7 troops crossing the river in a small boat. He ordered his No. 2 to give the target a burst as he bombed but before this was possible the boat had been lost to sight. Three staffing runs completed the operation and these produced a large fire. A pilot of another squadron which was in the area earlier in the day reported a tank in MINLANTAZEIK and, accordingly, this was searched for. However, nothing was seen and dense jungle in this particular locality rendered observation extremely difficult.[6]

---

6. TNA, AIR 27/376.

These sorties continued into early August until the Allies had cleared the area of Japanese. In July, Angus carried out ten sorties, sometimes two a day, often of three-hour duration. One can only imagine the sweat pouring off these pilots as they flew around in the humid, overcast sky in poor visibility, waiting for targets from the controllers. Add in the fact that they too were not often in the best health yet many were still determined to fly.

The medical statement at the end of July for the squadron confirms the loss of two pilots, sadly both due to flying accidents, but the interesting part is what the pilots were having to go through from a disease and infection perspective. Flight Lieutenant Inglis, the Squadron Medical Officer, states:

> During the month there were no straightforward cases of Malaria, but it is interesting to note that three patients admitted to hospital – one with bacillary dysentery, two with hepatitis – were found to have M.T. parasites in the blood. These patients were on mepacrine, one tablet daily, and yet the parasite which is most influenced by mepacrine was still in circulation and malaria symptoms developed while in hospital. It would seem therefore that mepacrine is merely suppressive and does not keep the body free from plasmodium and that any upset of the normal metabolism will precipitate an attack. Under these circumstances, the present disciplinary measures in connection with malaria would appear unjustified . There were five further cases of infective hepatitus, but only in one instance was it possible to trace the connection between cases.

During August Angus flew regularly but the success was hampered yet again by the weather, low cloud and rain making it hard to reach targets and identify them, with the first success of the month being on the 3rd August when Angus was airborne as part of 'A' Flight for a three hour sortie:

> The month started off very badly. On the first operation of the month, 6 aircraft were sent out to attack the Japanese's positions on the railway embankment near ABYA. Unfortunately, the weather prevented them from reaching their target, nor was it possible to

make the alternative target, a body of some 200 Japs. In the village of TINUGYUNG. A second flight of 6 aircraft also went out on a similar job, but on receiving an adverse weather report en route, returned without accomplishing their mission.

The weather improved on the 3rd and 12 aircraft were able to make a successful sortie. Although briefed to bomb and strafe NYAUNGKASHE, the aircraft were diverted by the VCP 'PINSTAN' to SATTHWAGON. 'A' Flight took the southern end of the village and put all its bombs (with the exception of one hang up) in the target area. Subsequent strafing runs produced 2 large fires. 'B' Flight attacked the Paungyl Kyuang and obtained a heavy concentration on the target and started a fire strafing.

On the following day, the 4th, another neat attack was made on dug-in positions at NYAUNGKASHE. 'A' Flight observed slit trenches on top of the embankments at either side of the railway track and 10 bombs were dropped on these. Bashas in the neighbourhood were then strafed with unobserved results. 'B' flight went for dug-in positions to the north of the railway bridge and did some very accurate bombing. Pilots were of the opinion that all but four of the trenches had been destroyed. The flight also strafed bashas in the area but no results observed.

On the 5th, 6th and 7th of the month, the monsoon had us in its grip and no operations were possible, but an early start on the 8th enabled us to go out to TAANGALON where a very good attack was made by 12 aircraft, resulting in extensive damage and several bashas left smouldering. We were not to know at this time but this was the last offensive action by 34 Squadron in the Japanese campaign. The honour of dropping the last 2 bombs fell to Sgt. Littlewood.

On the tenth of the month vague news was heard over the wireless to the effect that the total capitulation of the Japanese was to be expected at any moment. In spite of this however, the war still seemed to be carrying on and the Army had several jobs for us to do on the days following. Unfortunately, the weather on the 10th and 11th was very bad and permitted no flying whatsoever. (This was, perhaps, a good job because after our rather premature victory celebrations no-one felt inclined to do any serious work).

On the 12th August, 12 aircraft went out in support of the Army but because of heavy storms encountered en route they had to call the job off and returned to base.

By now it had become very apparent that the war really was coming to an end. No more offensive operations were carried out, but all aircraft were standing by with bombs 'just in case'. During this period the squadron moved south to ZAYATKWIN.

The final surrender of the Japanese having been negotiated, we took upon ourselves a new role of dropping leaflets. These were of various types according to whether they were intended for the local inhabitants of Jap occupied areas, isolated groups of the enemy who had received no official notifications of the surrender, or the guards of Jap POW camps.

Angus had been in action for a little over a month, but it was a very intense period of action with risks a-plenty. Fortunately, despite the odds being stacked against the Thunderbolt pilots flying from rough strips in heavily-laden aircraft – basically a flying bomb – they had few fatalities, only two through flying accidents and none through enemy action.

The flying though was as tough as it gets, with awful weather and hot humid conditions to contend with on sorties of up to three hours at a time. Dehydration and fatigue were constant enemies as well as malaria and dysentery. He was posted out of 34 Squadron during September of 1945 but that was not the end of his love affair with flying as you will read.

Angus eloquently puts his story across. He has created a fantastic autobiography which will serve as a fitting tribute to all those aircrew who served in the Far East and also those who flew the Thunderbolt II.

Acknowledgements

This book would not have come to fruition without the help and generosity of the following individuals: John Gadd, who had the foresight to record Angus' experiences in the first place; Richard Knight, for introducing me to John Gadd; and Andrew Thomas for his support and guidance with the images, as well as information on the operation of Thunderbolts in Burma during the Second World War.

Mark Hillier

Chapter 1

King and Country

About forty-two years ago, six P-47 Thunderbolts of No. 34 Fighter Bomber Squadron RAF took off from an airstrip in Burma. I was with them making my first operational flight.

The leading aircraft made a slow wide turn so that the rest of us could get into position, then in close formation we flew back over our base. I came to enjoy this moment because it was done for the benefit of those on the ground who looked after us and our aircraft so well. I saw it as a kind of salute to them, a good way to start the day's work. These six, beautiful aircraft, that belonged to them as much as to us, now roaring back across the airstrip.

Forty-two years ago that was and I wish I could do it again now. Mind you, a little earlier that day I wasn't feeling so elated. As we taxied up to the take-off end of the airstrip, I clearly remember how thoroughly scared I felt and that was a nasty shock, entirely unexpected, like a sudden revelation that I really wasn't cut out for this sort of thing. Perhaps this was something that happened to people going into action for the first time, the realization that you are about to make yourself a target for someone who wants to destroy you. The fact that we had been waiting two hours or more since our briefing may have had something to do with it, two hours of tension and intense excitement, wondering what it was all going to be like. The thought of firing those eight, big machine-guns for instance ; in training only one had been loaded. You could just hear it remotely, like the sound of a pneumatic drill down the road, and a slight tremor came through the airframe.

I think by the time we climbed into our aircraft I'd blown a few fuses and leaked a lot of adrenalin but now, strapped in and sitting with a thumb of a gloved hand on the energiser switch, everything was fine. We wore gloves because the aircraft got so hot you could burn yourself badly. Another precaution was the band of Vaseline across your forehead to stop the sweat running into your eyes.

I looked along the line of Thunderbolts to where the formation leader would give the signal to start engines and there it was, a clenched fist held high, stand-by, contact. Down it came and the snarl of the energisers made six engines give a great, whaling noise which gradually increased to a scream. Now the switch was moved in the opposite direction to the engage position and the scream ended abruptly in a heavy grunt and the four-bladed propeller began to turn, each blade six feet long. Round it went, the valves in the cylinder heads making urgent gasping noises. Then whoosh, away she went, bursting into a rich roaring note. Lovely, exciting noises they were. Smoke came swirling back in a hot blast past the cockpit, streams of flames sometimes if the engine had been a bit slow in picking up. Beautiful moments these. That gnawing bit of fear was now completely banished and I was never troubled with it again. There was anxiety at times – yes, a lot of that – but never again that useless nauseating fear.

Now it was time for take-off and I didn't much like the first part of this.

During training we practiced short take-offs and this technique seemed to abuse the aeroplane. Holding the stick hard back to keep the tail down, brakes fully on, the throttle was opened up and the aircraft quivered and shook horribly as the power built up and then, when the brakes couldn't hold it any longer, you let go and the aircraft lurched forward.

A Thunderbolt could use a mile of smooth runway for take-off quite easily but there were no smooth runways in Burma and with a full load of fuel, bombs and ammunition it was this short take-off drill every time. Even then it seemed to stick to the ground for ages. Airstrips were covered in a kind of bituminous material, 'felt Bithess' it was called, and sometimes this was supplemented by interlocking steel plates with rows of holes about the size of a snooker ball.

The holes would be for lightness as well as for drainage because all such material, in fact everything we used, had been flown in by transport aircraft. So, after the rather rough take-off, it was a relief to find yourself airborne getting your undercarriage up as quickly as possible and watching your air speed creep up past the two hundred mark. Then you could turn to head for your place with the rest of the flight.

After that close formation run over the airstrip, we opened out into a loose battle formation which was easy to hold and gave you a chance to look round and get to know the countryside. This was baffling at first with its lack of distinctive features but gradually you developed a feel for it. There were other things to be done as you flew along: routine checks of instruments, engine temperatures and pressures, fuel consumption and so on and of course you made a systematic search of the sky. It was unlikely at this stage we would meet enemy aircraft although the Japanese had used a routine that had produced surprises in the past.

Apparently deserted landing grounds were stocked and staffed, and aircraft would move up by stages from a considerable distance. Then they delivered a surprise attack and vanished. It was a good thing there were no hostile fighters when we were using Thunderbolts at low level.

In Europe, the American Thunderbolt pilots had a shock when they found themselves up against Focke-Wulf and Messerschmitt. P-47 loses were high and pilot morale was naturally low until they found the answer. For the very heavy but superbly streamlined Thunderbolt, the trick was to dive and zoom. A lighter aircraft was unable to hold them in a dive and the tables were turned when the Thunderbolt zoomed up for a height advantage – then dived to attack.

But, with the kind of altitudes we were confined to in Burma, there was, for the most part, no space for such tactics. The disappointing end to my first operational flight was an example of this.

As we flew further from our base, in the relatively dry zone of the central plain, two hundred miles from our target, the cloud cover both increased and lowered, pushing us down to about eight hundred feet. The rain became heavier and washed in a thick film over our cockpit canopies, while beneath us the paddy fields were lashed into a misty spume. Quite suddenly, the rained cleared, though the cloud base remained low. We flew on for a little while then it rapidly grew darker and ahead of us there was a wall of cloud like a cliff ; it looked incredibly solid. It was lit occasionally by flashes of lightening and, as we got nearer, the whole thing seemed to be swaying and twisting in columns of different colours: blackish brown, yellowy white, dark blue, grey. The effect of these sinister columns was theatrical as if watching from the front row of the dress circle, I was fascinated – then alarmed. Surely we weren't going to fly into this lot! It was probably something just like this that had caused the classic monsoon misfortune of the squadron that carried on regardless and lost nine out of their twelve aircraft.

I don't know if that is a true story but it was told to us as a cautionary tale. You didn't go into thick cloud if you could possibly avoid it although there were quite enough times when you couldn't. So, we turned back.

It had been a disappointing end to my first trip: I hadn't seen the enemy, hadn't even got near the enemy, although in a sense I suppose I had had a look at something that was a much more powerful enemy than the Japanese and that was the monsoon. It certainly destroyed far more aeroplanes. But this kind of abortive mission went much deeper than just disappointment. As a close support force, we were entirely committed to doing whatever we could to be of use to the Army. We knew and accepted that any call they made on us must be answered. There was no consolation in saying, 'Oh well, we can try again tomorrow.' We always had to try to get through and when we couldn't, we felt miserable for having failed them. These British, Indian and Nepalese troops were men of Bill Slim's Fourteenth Army later, known as the Thirty-Sixth Division.

It was an army with the rare distinction of having great unity and great affection for its commander. Its magnificent morale was infectious, and we were completely under its spell. Our admiration for the way they rose above the appalling conditions in which they lived and fought was boundless. We also knew, although not to the extent that was revealed later, that the enemy they were fighting was one of the most barbaric that the world had ever known. An enemy that could torture wounded men, use prisoners for bayonet practice, or burst into a hospital and find amusement in putting sick and injured patients to a slow death before turning their attention to the staff, doctors and nurses and doing the same to them.

In the North African campaign, there was respect for the enemy. In fact, it may be remembered that Rommel called that conflict 'a war without hate.' But for the Japanese there was no respect at all.

I should include in these thoughts mention of the Burmese people themselves: after all it was their country. They were fine people, good-humoured and likeable. In 1941, three weeks after the attack on Pearl Harbor, the Japanese bombed Rangoon. They used fragmentation bombs and caused seven thousand civilian casualties. For the next four and a half years, the Burmese had their country wrecked as it became a battle ground for the muddy footpath to India. The beautiful city of Mandalay was all but knocked to bits and countless temples and pagodas, with their little bells tinkling in the breeze, were also smashed. In many cases, I suppose the damage was irreparable. I don't know to what extent the Burmese were compensated for all this; perhaps they weren't.

I remember once we were briefed to attack a target consisting of pack animals including elephants. Well, I wasn't going to do it. The idea of not doing my duty was disturbing but there was a stronger sense of duty at work then. If you kill an animal, you do it cleanly. Machine-gunning a mass of bullocks, mules and elephants would leave many to die of horrible injuries. I felt a bit of a traitor but my bombs, for once, would fall wide and my guns would also miss the target. With luck, nobody would notice. But the point didn't arise, as the weather was too bad and we didn't take-off. A few days later an order came through that elephants were not to be destroyed: they took a long time to train and they would be needed when the teak industry got going again. I might also add that, a while back, leaflets had been dropped telling the Burmese to hide their animals so the Japanese couldn't use them and to take their bullock-carts to pieces for the same reason – but how do you hide an elephant?

Now, I have been talking about Burma and life on the Thunderbolt Squadron and there is more to be said in that direction but, as this is something of a flying autobiography, it should obey the rules and start at square one. So how did it all begin?

Well, it began when the RAF was permitted to start its expansion in the late thirties – and that was only just in time as we all know. The short service commission was devised to build up a solid core of highly-trained air crew. They wanted a lot of very fit and fairly well-educated young men and they went looking for them – advertising, visiting schools and so on. I was still a few years too young and, in other respects, I found myself very wide of the mark. I wasn't following the academic path that would enable me to sit an entrance examination with confidence. I was also inclined to hurl myself with a bit too much enthusiasm into exploits with horses, bicycles, ice skates – anything that offered scope for thrills and speed. The occasional accident that occurred had no lasting effect: the casualty department of the local hospital patched me up and after, a few weeks, I would be back in action.

Then something more serious happened and, combined with my academic limitations, it overshadowed my prospect of making the grade for RAF air crew. A heavy blow to the stomach caused a rupture. The hospital wanted to operate straight away but my parents would not agree. Instead I was lumbered with a truss and a bottle of water. I know that's an odd combination but I will explain in a moment.

As the late 1930s progressed, boys talked not so much of what jobs they would do when they left school but which service they would join. When they asked me I said I would join the Air Force. What as? As a pilot, of course.

This outrageous announcement was greeted with gallons of verbal cold water and withering looks. To the average schoolboy, the concept of an RAF pilot was little short of Superman. Did I realise how quickly you had to think – make calculations, that kind of thing? And then there was the medical: things like blowing up a tube of mercury and holding it at a certain level while your lungs almost burst and your eyes almost popped out of your head. There was Superman again and I didn't match up to that very well.

I was a tall skinny boy and quite strong, apart from the rupture. Later in life a friend said her first impression of me was a skeleton with a black eye! So, there were these two big barriers, education and health, and as time went by there appeared to be a third – my age. The war might come and go and I would be too young to take part in it. That, but for a few months, was almost true.

So, my ambition was right out in the cold with no guidelines and no encouragement. It was very much acceped in those days that young people should know their place. The formula was, start at the bottom get a proper grounding. You were looked at with alarm and mistrust if you were at all presumptuous in the matter of your potential, unless you had an expensive education, on the strength of which you could claim a head start. Half of my friends went to public schools, the other half to grammar or council schools. I was equally happy with both of them. We were not divided by the amount or absence of school fees; we respected each other's individuality.

The years passed and my thoughts of flying were little more than a dreamy, romantic hope. I think that the gap between how I actually saw myself and what I believed the Air Force required was so great that my ambition could only be quixotic. But I didn't lower my sights and accept that I might perhaps serve in a less demanding role. For me there was only one thing – fighter pilot.

It must have been in the late summer of 1938. The war seemed to be getting very near. I was still clinging to my hopes of becoming an RAF pilot but my plan had changed. I had begun with the thought of a five-year, short service commission followed by work on a leading newspaper, with the intention of becoming an overseas correspondent. My plan had also included learning a foreign language during my time with the RAF. Now, it was now simply – get ready for war.

That damned rupture, though, was becoming a real problem. A friend had told me that, even if the rupture healed, it would leave a permanent weakness that would be detected in the very thorough medical examination. However, I came across a full – page advertisement in the *Daily Sketch*. I believe it said, 'Important announcement for rupture sufferers,' and it gave details of a thing called 'The Brooks Appliance'. I even remember the price of 28s 6d.

The contraption I had been using had been made-to-measure by a surgical appliance shop – a heavy, old-fashioned truss that would have supported a horse with strength to spare. It caused blistering and was continuously slipping out of position so that the risk of a strangulated hernia was ever-present. Also, I had to regularly shove a hand down the top of my trousers to push it back into position and a clean shirt quickly got a grubby. Added to that I received frequent, suspicious glances from adults who probably thought I was brazenly attending to some pressing aspect of puberty.

When the person delivered my Brooks, device I was somewhat puzzled. The package was so small it might have contained a wristwatch. The makers claimed that it could be worn under swimming trunks and not be noticed, and they were right. Bless you Brooks! I was able to resume nearly all of my more strenuous activities. And the bottle of water I mentioned earlier – well that was a present from two old ladies who ran a newsagent's shop. I had seen a jigsaw puzzle in their window one day with an exciting picture of a Hawker Hart fighter. I had to have that, and they promised to keep it for me until I had saved enough money to buy it and, as they put it carefully away under the counter, they probably caught sight of the look in my eyes. One of them said, 'You like aeroplanes do you?'

'Yes,' I replied and I told them about my interest in joining the RAF if I was fit enough.

'You look like a very fit young man to me,' said the old lady. So, I explained about the rupture and then these two old dears looked at each other as if they knew something and one of them turned to me and said, 'We are off on holiday next week for a fortnight, but come and see us when we get back.'

In due course, I saw them again when I went to pay for the jigsaw. They passed it to me across the counter and something else. There was a little box nicely wrapped in blue paper, 'This is for you,' they said. 'We've been to Lourdes, dear, and brought you back this little bottle of water. Use it like a lotion.'

I thanked them and went on my way with the Hawker Hart jigsaw in one hand and the Lourdes water in the other. It took a long time to use up all the water – just wetting my finger tip and rubbing it on before going to bed each night – but I decided that, when the last drop had gone, I would go to the doctor. And it was quite exciting when the day eventually arrived when I tipped the bottle upside down and found there was nothing left.

That appointment with the doctor must have been one of the most significant moments of my life. He spent quite a time over his examination. Eventually, he shook his head and said, 'There's no rupture there.' That, in itself was excellent news but better still he added, 'In fact I can't believe you ever were ruptured.' With grateful thanks to the Brooks partnership I went on my way feeling much relieved and splendidly happy.

Preparations for war increased. There was a practice black-out one evening and this novelty brought the crowds out in force for the rather negative satisfaction of not being able to see anything. One of my quick-witted friends called for me and said this was the ideal opportunity to raid an orchard he had had his eye on. Well I felt that to be a squalid waste of an interesting experience so instead I walked along the top promenade on the seafront with some less inquisitive friends. It was not yet dark though the sun had been set some time and we walked along chatting about the changes we might expect to see in wartime.

There was an atmosphere of excitement mingled with apprehension. Somebody shouted, 'Look!' and people hurried to the railings and started looking towards the west. We joined them and then we saw it too. A thrilling and totally unexpected surprise ; two formations of fighter aircraft flying in low over the sea – Spitfires or Hurricanes, I didn't know the difference then. From where we stood we were above them and able to see the helmeted heads of the pilots as these beautiful, sleek fighter planes flew past, filling the air with that rich pulsating rhythm that only a large formation of piston engine aircraft can make. These days, young boys have seen films and television and actual air displays which make the sight of aircraft nothing extraordinary, but for me this was a fantastic experience. I had never seen aeroplanes so close or so marvellously presented. All the threads of my ambition and longing came together, consummated in those few, superb moments. Now I knew that what I had just seen had to be for me.

When the war started I joined the Air Raid Precautions (ARP), later called the Civil Defence, and I joined as a messenger. Already some of the older boys from my school were already in the Air Force or Fleet Air Arm; one or two were also in the Army, of course.

I should have sat my final exams in the summer of 1940 but my school days ended abruptly. It's a remarkable fact that we had, in England, quite a number of people who actually hoped for a German victory. Many of these were absurdly obvious sort of minor spies, who were rounded up very easily. I saw a man at the time the invasion was expected being bundled into a Black Maria. He was carrying a huge camera with a wooden case and brass fittings and he had a conspicuously continental bicycle with fat tyres. His dress was also very continental and he looked exactly like Goebbels, the Nazi Propaganda Minister. Then again there was a butcher in the town who had a German wife who was found to have vast stocks of tinned meat stored away in readiness for the invaders. But these were people with actual ties to Germany. It came as something of a shock to find fellow Englishmen in the enemy camp.

There was a boy at my school who quite opening professed his support for Nazi Germany. During private study periods, he sat at his desk writing little notes which he then folded and placed in his pocket. He had a bottle of ink in front of him and he wrote with what was known as the relief nib which enabled him to produce a distinctly German or Gothic script.

On the pretext of wanting to fill my fountain pen, I crept up silently and although he quickly slapped a hand over the paper on his desk, I had seen enough. Another sixth form boy was the son of a police inspector and I asked him to tell his father about this state of affairs. I now knew that our Nazi classmate was paying the younger boys to spend their weekends collecting details of invasion defences. Those bits of paper decorated with little swastikas were payslips. I caught sight of the words, 'For Services to the Third Reich. Heil Hitler'. I also knew that he had a Gestapo style arrangement for dealing with people who interfered. I came across one such incident in the cloakroom and put a instant stop to it.

A few days later, cycling home from school, I put on my brakes as I approached a crossroad at the bottom of the steep hill – and nothing happened. I just went whizzing on. When I eventually coasted to a stop, I found that the nuts holding the cable ends had been slackened off. My police contact told me he had spoken to his father who said they would need evidence – so evidence they should have.

As we jostled out of the classroom one day, I slipped a hand into the young Nazi's pocket and found what I wanted. Police reaction was very quick. My desk was by a window and the next morning I saw two, black, police cars come briskly up the drive. They stopped at the administrative building and a group of policemen went inside. A little later, someone came hurrying across to our classroom, whispered to the master-in-charge and then called the little Nazi to go with him. I watched as he was driven away in one of the police cars. His house was searched and quantities of Nazi propaganda were found; apparently this material was sent via Italy which had not at that time entered the war.

An unusual item for those days was also found, a radio transmitter. About a week after all this excitement, the headmaster referred to the matter one morning in assembly. He said that the boy concerned had been very foolish and he now realised this and was sorry. The headmaster then went on to say that it was most unfortunate that someone had seen fit to regard this as a matter for the police and that this had caused a lot of unnecessary fuss. Understandably, the headmaster was annoyed because he was a close friend of the Nazi boy's family and was frequently entertained at their home.

A few weeks later I was involved in some prank and had to report to the headmaster's study. Boys in the sixth form were not usually caned ; they were assumed to have grown out of that and a reprimand was usually seen as sufficient punishment. Well, the head was sitting at his desk when I went in and he ignored me for some little time, turning the pages of a *National Geographic* magazine. I stood gazing over the top of his head at the window behind him. Eventually he said quietly, 'Ah yes, Findon.' Then he got up, walked slowly across the room to a cupboard, and from this he took out a cane. He pointed with it to a leather armchair in front of the fire. 'Bend over there,' he said. I had been caned pretty hard before but this, as well as being very painful, was also frightening. I lost count of the number of strokes.

I was later told by people who were walking past the building

that they could hear this beating fifty yards away. It seemed the man had gone mad. He was lashing out wildly and I was afraid my back might be damaged – and of course it was important to me to remain fit. This threat to my health, and all that implied, maddened me. I struggled up.

It was difficult to stand but I got up, turned and cried out, 'You bloody fool!'

The headmaster shouted, 'Get down!' and pushed me onto the chair and started to beat me again. I somehow managed to get up once more and get out of the door. I slid along the wall in the corridor as best I could reeling from the pain.

One of the younger masters then came by and said uneasily, 'Are you alright Findon?' His voice seemed a long, long way off. Then he said, 'Oh good God! Can I help you?' I shook my head and as soon as I heard him walk away I walked on. It was raining outside. I got my bike and mac from the cloakroom and, leaning on the saddle, I left for home. I didn't put the raincoat on. The rain felt very soothing running down my skin. So ended my school days. I never went back.

It should be understood that in those days it was unthinkable that a boy should swear at any adult as I had done, let alone a headmaster. Indeed I had surprised even myself. Yet looking back, I think the man had so lowered himself that all respect had gone. I felt no remorse.

It was a simple matter to change from part to full-time Civil Defence duty. I took a job at the control centre and with my pay I was able to buy various text books, books on aircraft recognition and so on and put together an objective training programme. We were having very few air raids at the time and, wanting to do something more useful for the war effort, after a few months I changed my job.

Food production was obviously very important at the time, and I started work with the War Agriculture Executive Committee as a tractor ploughman. There was three months training on the job then, for most of the time, I would be on my own. Huge areas of the South Downs were being put to plough. The foreman's instructions were simple. He would just point to some distant speck and say, 'Up to there and across to there,' and that was my week's work mapped out. With a twelve-mile bike ride to and from work, I became very fit and the whole thing was extremely satisfying as well as useful.

Ploughing was fascinating. To keep a furrow straight and at the right depth, called for constant attention. Often, on a tricky bit of ground, I would become so absorbed in my work that I didn't notice the time and it might be as late as three in the afternoon before I stopped for my lunch of bread and cheese. But, above all, this was a time of preparation for the Air Force. My training plan continued even while driving the tractor, when I could conveniently divide my attention between the work and something such as the Morse Code which I had difficulty in learning and I did this while I ploughed.

Who would have thought, seeing that lone tractor chugging across the Downs, that the driver was sitting there saying, 'Dah dit de dah dit dah de dah,' and so on. But at other times I would have an aircraft recognition booklet fixed to the tractor with a clothes peg and I would be noting dihedral angles, aspect ratios, leading trailing edge angles and dozens of other things. Aircraft recognition was a wonderful way to develop powers of observation and it serves me well even now.

You might think that working on top of the Downs was a good place for seeing a variety of aircraft, but you won't see a ploughman staring up at the sky: that's not the way straight furrows are made. Also, one just never heard an aeroplane: the tractor engine drowned out every other sound, which probably explains why, one day, I saw the unfamiliar sight of an ambulance bumping over a downland track in the distance. A German fighter had strafed a ploughman's tractor and a cannon shell had smashed the top of the radiator; a piece of it had flown back and decapitated the man.

As well as working on the land by day, I had joined the Home Guard. Details of Germany's Operation *Sealion,* as it was called – the proposed invasion of Britain – were making themselves known. So now I had guard duty on one night in four, weekend training exercises, invasion false alarms, night exercises and so on.

The Home Guard spirit was magnificent, one of the great experiences of my life, but with candles being burnt at both ends, I would often change my Home Guard uniform for my tractor clothes as the sun was rising and back into uniform as it set. Sometimes this got a bit too much for me and I would stop my tractor and lie on the earth beside it and steal an hour's sleep.

When winter came, the work switched from ploughing to land clearance. Hooking a cable onto the back of the tractor, small trees such as hawthorn were pulled out. A gang of agricultural labourers were provided for this and I used to travel to and from work on the transport that was laid on for them. One day the lorry that came was simply a flat-bed truck with no sides and no tailboard, the kind used for carrying sacks of grain. There were patches of ice on it too. The same lorry came for us at the end of the day and we made a strong protest to the driver. The next morning there it was again. I heard a woman at the nearby bus stop say, 'Oh dear look at those poor men.'

Some of the labourers were old and very poor. Walking up the hill behind one of them at the end of the day's work I watched the sleet melting on his bare back where there were holes in his clothes. The lorry driver told us it was difficult to get a covered vehicle but if we liked to pass the hat round at the end of the week when we got our wage packets he would see what he could do.

By next morning I had an idea and, as we stood waiting for the lorry, I said to the men, 'If that open one comes again don't get on it. We will take a bus to County Hall and I will speak for the lot of us.' Their foreman, Ernie, was one of those loyal, long-suffering men for whom I had great admiration but whose sense of duty can be sadly exploited. He spoke out against me. He told the group, 'Don't you men go listening to no trouble-maker now. Let young Angus thar do what he wants but you come along with me.'

The lorry arrived with the same flat top and so did a nice warm bus. I glanced at the foreman and he met my gaze. There was a firm and defiant look in his old blue eyes. I said to him, 'I'm sorry Ernie. I've got to do this.' Then I took hold of the handrail of the bus and said, 'Come on lads – County Hall.'

One of them raised a cheer and they all trooped aboard. We watched that flat-topped grain lorry drive away with poor old Ernie sitting all alone like a ship-wrecked sailor.

At County Hall, we waited for the staff to arrive, then I went in and put the case to a senior official. He was seated at his desk, well-groomed, tidy with collar and tie. I was standing there, weather – beaten, with rough, heavy out – door clothing. My request was approved without any fuss at all. A bell was rung and an office girl came in and took the petty cash slip which the man handed to her. Our bus fares were refunded, plus payment for the remainder of our journey. We were guaranteed proper transport from that day on.

As we walked up the track to our little wood, we passed a group of land-girls. Obviously they had queried Ernie's lone arrival and had been told the reason. Now they booed us heartily and cried, 'Shame!' I would have done the same and I was glad of this as I felt it might be of some comfort to the old foreman.

The time came when I could volunteer for Air Crew duties, but I hesitated. Already five boys from the local scene, three in the R.A.F. and two in the Fleet Air Arm, had been killed. The father of one was a fellow Home Guard and he suddenly seemed to age very rapidly. I knew his son's wife too – a lovely girl, very jolly. She always seemed to be smiling and laughing. Recently, I had passed her in the street, dressed in black, her face very pale and she gave me a little smile. The Wellington Bomber her husband had piloted was damaged over Germany and on landing it had burst into flames. The rear gunner was unconscious but this man had got him out together with the rest of the crew, but he left it too late to escape himself. The fabric had burnt off the outside of the fuselage and he was seen struggling towards one of the forward hatches, on fire from head to foot. He had been one of the few boys at school who knew my great ambition and always gave me encouragement. I felt awfully sad about his death – I still do. News also came of the death of a near relative, another Wellington pilot. His aircraft was shot down over France. I felt it might be tactless to come in one day and say, 'Guess what. I have just joined the R.A.F.' But then again, why not?

With war, inevitably, comes grief. So, after a discreet interval I went ahead and, feeling a bit guilty, I sneaked off to the local recruiting office and got the ball rolling. I couldn't keep it secret for long because I had to go to London for the selection board and that took three days.

There I was at last, in December 1941, blowing up the lung capacity machine – on reflection I have had more difficulty blowing up balloons at children's parties. The medical exam proved to be no problem and I was smiling to myself as the doctor worked his fingertips very slowly and carefully over my stomach. By then I had a Rolls-Royce of a stomach. I was also glad that the scars from my beating at the hands of the headmaster had faded away: scars from a flogging can be bad for a man's character.

The written tests came next and here my performance was not impressive. It would have made more sense to join the Air Training Corps but that would have meant leaving the Home Guard. I had built up a great allegiance there and, if there had been an invasion and I had left them, I could never have forgiven myself.

The selection board frowned as they looked at my results. I was obviously a borderline case. One officer shot some mental arithmetic questions at me and by sheer luck I got them right. He looked at my papers again and observed that I had left school some time ago; I was, no doubt, a bit rusty.

'What's the square root of 144?' said one of the others. I got that one right too.

The president of the board looked uneasy. It seemed that I needed a little more than the square root of 144 to be accepted for air crew training. He sat, turning over the stack of papers in front of him – it's surprising how much bumf they can build up on a chap in three days. I watched him intently. There was a terrible silence in the room. Suddenly, he seemed to relax. He had come to the point where sports and hobbies were listed. I had been worried about that. I couldn't put down any team games, of course, as I had been unable to participate due to the rupture. But a smile now came over the president's face and a corresponding feeling of relief came over me.

'I see you ride,' he said.

'Yes, Sir.'

'You like horses do you?' I saw signs of progress here.

'Oh very much so, yes.'

Now the president looked like a man who had just solved a very difficult puzzle. With a brief glance and a little nod to his colleagues on either side, he said, 'Well then, we think you will make a pilot. You are accepted.'

I have thought many times since, just how pleasant it must be for a selection board to see a young man so filled with such immense happiness and gratitude.

We air crew candidates were now assembled in batches in a small room and sworn in. We were given a silver lapel badge with R.A.F.V.R. written on it and that would have to be returned when we started our training. There was no indication when that would be. We just knew it was unlikely to be very soon. So I went back to my land work and Home Guard duties.

When I was sent to work on a farm near Hastings, I had some further involvement with the Nazi element. It had never occurred to me to regard the people I was working with as anything unusual, yet some of them were not at all agricultural. Neither of course was I. Quite a few of them were clearly under some form of directive owing to them being conscientious objectors and that manifested itself in several ways. For instance, at odd moments when you were changing engine oil or greasing the tractor, it would be normal to pass the time of day with your colleagues – but not at this place. Here nobody spoke to me and I received a lot of dark glances. There was just one man who was friendly. He was a genuine farmhand who looked after the cows and he alone would smile and say hallo to me.

One day he said he had heard I was a Home Guard and that I was also going to fly in the R.A.F. He then looked round cautiously and said quietly, 'There's funny things going on round here, like up in the old farmhouse. Don't ask me how I know but there is wireless equipment up there, and people comes late at night and talks to Germans.' He went on to say that he was in the local Home Guard and he had told his platoon commander, but he wasn't taken seriously.

I felt sorry for the man when he explained, 'I know I am a dopey-looking fellow and they think I am simple you see – but I knows its true.' He was right about the dopey part of it. He had a turnip-shaped head and wore steel-rimmed spectacles with thick round lenses. An ill-fitting Home Guard uniform would have done little to improve the image.

He continued, 'What's going on up there – it ain't right.' Then he asked if I would see my Home Guard commander and get something done about it. I promised I would do whatever was necessary to have the situation investigated but I never heard the outcome because just then my R.A.F. papers arrived and my work on the land was at an end.

One of the more surly and hitherto silent men in that strange collection couldn't resist having a go at me on my last day. He was waiting in the tractor shed and as I drove in and switched off my engine he ambled up and said, So you are off to fight Churchill's war for him, are you?'

I told him, 'Not just Churchill's war – Our war.' He then began to rant and rail at me with a kind of mad hate in his eyes. He asked if I realised that one day I would be ordered to machine-gun my fellow countrymen. I suppose he was alluding to some remote possibility of a revolution or a civil war. His mind was horribly poisoned by something, though nothing he said bothered me. He was just a bore. I turned away without answering I went off to start my training.

The Air Crew Receiving Centre (A.C.R.C. or less respectfully 'arcy-tarcy') was at Lord's Cricket ground. It was a most impressive, though quite unenjoyable example of administrative organisation. In the space of a week we were kitted out, documented, vaccinated, inoculated, inspected and generally chased about at speeds we would not have believed possible. We therefore looked forward, with desperate longing, to Saturday afternoon when we might be free of this relentless pressure for just a little while. So, we were naturally upset at being told we had to be on parade at 14.00 hours on the Saturday afternoon. Nobody knew what it was about and there was a lot of discontented muttering as we fell in. As we marched away, I glanced back and it seemed the whole R.A.F. was on the move, flight after flight marching along.

'Keep eyes to the front !' shouted a sharp-eyed corporal and on we went, 'Right, left, right, left etc. Our mood didn't improve when we discovered the reason for the unscheduled parade.

The march ended in an open-air theatre in Regent's Park and it quickly became clear that we were being press-ganged into being film extras. Row upon row of us, seated tier above tier in a large semi-circle. A plump, little American with a cigar sticking out of the centre of his mouth climbed onto the stage, removed the cigar and said, 'Ok fellows. Now this is what

I want you to do.' He waved a hand, 'One, two, three – "We'll meet again, don't know where, don't know when." You get it? You're going to make a movie with Miss Vera Lynn. You guys are going to sing the chorus.'

With all too obvious reluctance, we ran through it once. Then there was a delay while various stand-ins were put in front of the mike, and cameras and lights were adjusted. We became even more restless. Our NCOs seemed to have vanished and there were no officers in sight. The film makers were trying to calm things down and George Formby was sent onto the stage. He played his banjo and sang a couple of numbers but there was no applause – we just sat in silence. He looked a little bemused and, without further ado, he left the stage.

The American film man got on stage once again and asked us for just one more chorus. The cameras began to turn and there were a few obliging voices but gradually these were drowned out by a refrain that grew to an overwhelming volume as it was taken up by everyone of us.

'We'll meet again, don't know where, don't know when. On land or sea, you will always hear me, singing this song. Show me the way to go home, yeah, show me the way to go home. I'm tired and I want to go to bed.'

I don't know if they got any useful footage out of this captive audience, but I do know that the title of 'Forces Sweetheart' was not bestowed on Miss Lynn by us. We felt quite annoyed with our Air Ministry masters for allowing this to happen. We hadn't joined the Air Force to be used by pop stars.

The work of the Air Crew Receiving Centre was soon complete. It had equipped us and set us up – albeit very basically – as airmen. We were then sent to the Elementary Training Wing (E.T.W.) where we had to endure a kind of toughening-up course. That was at a camp near Ludlow in Shropshire. I'll just share one last memory of 'arcy-tarcy' though. I was told one day there was going to be a pay parade: this shows how naïve I was. I said, 'What do you mean pay? We get our food, a uniform and ammunition and we're here to fight the enemy – so what's this about pay? We don't need pay surely.'

They said, 'Yes of course you do. You get paid.'

We went on parade and the paying officer slapped down a pound in front of me which I stared at. It looked quite absurd – a pound and a soap coupon. I saluted, picked it up and went on my way. That was the sort of 'King and Country' approach I had to things then.

Chapter 2

L.A.C. Findon, Pilot

My next posting was the real thing – the Initial Training Wing. I was sent to No.3 ITW at Torquay. We had an odd distinction in our dress there. I think that this was the only time this happened in the R.A.F. During duty hours, we wore white shirts in the summer months. We also had to blanco, to gleaming white, our blue webbing belts. That had to be done every day and the brasses polished. Quite a tricky job it was to stop the metal polish touching the white belt. Naturally, boots shone and buttons sparkled. Incidentally, we had to buy our own polish – so I suppose it was a good thing that we got a pound a week!

ITW was a sort of aircrew trainee university. We were taught to be extremely smart – no fancy bull, just plain, brilliant smartness. We quickly learnt to take a pride in ourselves and, above all, to settle in quickly to our studies to prepare for the vital examinations that lay ahead.

The staff there were all marvellous people. They displayed a tremendous degree of dedication, and every one of them was a man you could respect. We even had our own ITW marching song (I think this was the work of an ex-BBC man). Occasionally the order was given, 'March at ease,' and this was the signal for our arms not to swing quite so high but more particularly to sing – and away we'd go, 'They gave us a belt to bullshit and a couple of pair of boots, for one must be white and one must be black, but nobody cares two hoots. OH! ITW, ITW,' … and so on. We worked hard and we worked happily.

I have a magnificent memory of the Chief Ground Instructor who took us for navigation. He was a Welshman and one of the most perfectly balanced people I have ever met. His rank of Wing Commander meant little: he was, by his personal gifts and development, way above man-made rank and he would have had just as much admiration and respect from us had he been a corporal. He was quite a small man but absolutely devoid of any inhibitions on this account. He was a first-class lecturer and the mysteries and skills of navigation were always beautifully delivered. In contrast to most of my school days, I was now thoroughly enjoying learning. The only thing I feared was that something unforeseen would delay my progress – and it did. Following the celebration of victory in our inter-squadron sports event with an evening on the beer at the Drum Inn at Covington, the officer who came with us said, 'We don't want any thick heads tomorrow so we will start the day with a swim in the harbour at 06.00 hours.'

We walked back to Torquay through heavy rain that night, and next morning I didn't feel too good – something a bit more than just last night's beer. Anyway, I showed willing and dived into the harbour.

I felt worse during the day, and that evening we had barrack-room sports. That was when the whole building was scrubbed and polished from top to bottom. By that time, I felt really rough. My room-mate, Gerry Hill, a country boy from Sunderland, told the duty sergeant who said that I should report sick the following morning. Fortunately, Gerry didn't leave it at that. He took it upon himself to bring round an orderly from sick quarters and I very quickly found myself in an ambulance, on the way to hospital with a dose of pneumonia.

Thinking of that harbour at Torquay reminds me of a sad little incident. We used to do dinghy drill which could be rather uncomfortable on a chilly, autumn day. You pulled on a soaking, wet uniform – unless of course you were the first – soggy boots and all, then a Mae West. You plummeted down to the water and there you got yourself into a fighter dinghy. Now we had with us a strapping great lad, an Orkney Islander, who said he didn't want to do this because he was sure he would drown. 'Nonsense,' he was told, 'that's exactly why you should do it. It will give you confidence in your equipment. Now jump!' said the sergeant. Reinforcing the order with a hefty nudge, he sent this lad hurtling down to the water.

We were dismayed to see that following the great splash, the poor chap didn't come to the surface, only an empty Mae West: it hadn't been laced up. The top of the boy's head was visible for a moment then he sank again. 'Dinghy !' someone shouted, but the dinghy that normally stood by during these exercises was some distance away, the oarsman probably thinking that they weren't any more jumps to come. Luckily, there was an ex-Glasgow policeman among us with experience of life-saving and he plunged in and rescued the boy.

At the end of ITW came those vital examinations. On passing these you were reclassified from Aircraftman 2nd Class to Leading Aircraftman. Then you got your 'props', that is to say the two-bladed, propeller badge to sew onto the sleeve of your tunic and a pay increase to 7/6d a day – but above all, you were now about to fly.

Ahead lay the aptitude or grading course with up to twelve hours on Tiger Moths. My first flight didn't make a very good impression on me. I had always thought of flying as something in which smoothness, speed and a sense of freedom, plus a bird's eye view of the ground, would all be paramount. We bumped along, accompanied by a frenzied blaring noise and we seemed to stagger uncertainly into the air, at which point the gusty conditions buffeted us so much that any idea of smoothness was totally absent. As for speed, there wasn't very much of that and of the ground beneath, only a tiny amount could be seen, the rest obstructed by the aeroplane framework.

Had this been a peacetime sortie, I think that on landing I would have scarpered and spent my money on a motorcycle or a decent horse. Galloping a steeple-chaser was infinitely more exhilarating. But of course, my subsequent flights became much more interesting and increasingly challenging. Though I was probably on my way to the realisation that flying was not an end in itself, it was what one could do with an aeroplane that really appealed to me – apart from the sheer, unadulterated bliss of flying an enchanting and beautiful aeroplane such as one of the earlier marks of Spitfire.

The grading school was at Ansty near Coventry. It was the depths of winter and, with the industrial haze of the midlands, good flying conditions were hard to find; that is to say a clear horizon and a cloud base not too low. You cannot teach someone to fly without a reasonably good horizon.

The Chief Instructor flew first thing each morning to check the weather and, on his return, he would dive low over the airfield, throw a handkerchief out of the cockpit then zoom up to circuit height, where he would close the throttle and glide round in silence making a perfect, three-point landing on top of that little white blob painted on the grass. 'How could anyone be as good as that?' I wondered. My attempts at landing were not that good: I just hadn't got the idea of rounding out at the correct height, then getting the stick back, little by little, at just the right moment to achieve a three-point landing. I just bounced horribly.

The final test came, and I felt I that had made a total mess of it. I ran through the required exercises, trying my very best to remember everything that I had learned – then the examiner instructed me to fly back to base, join the circuit and land. He said this in a very calm and relaxed manner and I responded with unbecoming exuberance. I had kept careful note of our position in relation to the airfield ; it was always embarrassing for a pupil to have to say, 'Yes sir. Which way should we be going?'

I tipped the aircraft on its side, pulled round in a tight turn, surprising myself by doing two things I had not yet been taught, and shoved the nose hard down and dived towards Ansty. The wind whistled beautifully through the rigging wires and, as the airspeed rose, I pulled back the throttle to control the engine revs. It was like suddenly playing the opening bars of a concerto after plugging away at scales, day after day.

Very dryly, the examiner's voice came into my earphones, 'Findon, who taught you to lose height like that?'

Quickly I brought the nose up, 'Oh, nobody sir. Sorry sir.' It seemed an awful long time before the speed came down to an acceptable figure. When, eventually, we were descending sedately towards Ansty in the approved style, I sat there feeling guilty of some dreadful misdemeanour. Ahead lay the landing.

We bounced across the ground in my usual clumsy manner and the examiner said, 'You haven't quite got the landing, have you Findon?' That was putting it very nicely.

'No, sir. Not quite.'

Preoccupied with the importance of this test, I hadn't noticed that I was feeling a bit odd. I called in at the Station Sick Quarters and was immediately sent to bed with a high temperature and other signs of flu. I don't know whether that had helped or hindered my flying. It could have helped by relaxing me: it was usual to be horribly tense and nervous on these occasions, and the uninhibited way I had flung that Tiger Moth

L.A.C. Findon, Pilot 23

Angus's 'You are going to be a pilot' booklet. A note that he wrote states, 'We were given this at a great assembly in a Manchester cinema when the result of our grading course at Ansty was announced. We were told that our number and name would be called out, together with the role for which we had been selected. Those not selected for pilot training were to answer, "Sir, I understand ". The rest simply answered, "Sir". Having failed to solo at Ansty, I braced myself for disappointment. Then the voice said, "1806476, L.A.C. Findon, Pilot." My imense happiness was only spoilt by the awful disappointment that some of the other chaps had to face. Some of the course did not mind at all. They had no desire to become "Drivers, airframe". (*John Gadd Collection*)

around was far from the orthodox manner normally presented to an examiner. My relaxed state could have been interpreted as a shocking indifference to flying discipline, in which case there was no future for me as a pilot.

I now had to wait several, agonising weeks for the result. We went on leave with the wretched uncertainty of the crucial results hanging over everything. We then reported to the great transit camp at Heaton Park, Manchester in all its winter bleakness.

Soon after arrival, we assembled in the cinema to hear the results of our grading course. We were told that our names would be read out together with the role for which we had been selected. Those selected for pilot training would simply answer, 'Sir,' while those for other aircrew categories would say, 'Sir, I understand.' So, under my breath, I practiced saying, 'Sir, I understand,' so if I had to say it, I would get it right and not reveal my disappointment. I hadn't long to wait, being the letter 'F'.

'1800476 L.A.C. Findon, Pilot.'

A sudden elation almost struck me dumb. 'Sir,' I managed to say. I tried not to hear the flat, disappointed voices of those who had to reply, 'Sir, I understand'. In many cases it didn't mean they wouldn't have made good pilots, but they would make better navigators or some other aircrew category.

The tedious weeks of waiting for a boat to take us to Canada to start our flying training dragged by so slowly. Transit camps can be such awfully dreary places. Then suddenly, with no warning, there was a great buzz of activity. We rushed into action, packed our kit and one night boarded a blacked-out train and trundled our way through the darkness.

Next morning, we found ourselves in Liverpool where we boarded the *Queen Elizabeth* and she took us across the Atlantic to New York. I sailed in five troop ships during the war and the *Q.E.* I liked the least; she was simply too big at 30,000 tons. A more reasonable 10,000 tons was not too small to make for an enjoyable voyage and it was easier to find your way around.

The Q.E. had a staff of N.C.Os who made life as unpleasant as they could. They were rather like the 'arcy-darcy' crowd and I fell foul of one of them on the first night in board. I was found on my bunk with my boots off. I had never occurred to me that in time of war you should keep your boots on all the time on a ship.

We were organised into watches and I was put to guard the ship's brig. There was nobody in it so this was a lonely vigil which grew lonelier as time went by and it became clear that they had forgotten all about me. From my Home Guard days, I knew you should never leave your post, so I stayed there, in this gloomy part of the ship with its cold, metal floor and heavy, rivetted, steel walls. After some twelve hours, I heard footsteps in the distance and attracted the attention of a cleaner who reported my plight and I was relieved.

Without exception, food on troop ships was inadequate and all but inedible. It seemed very strange to sit in the beautiful dining saloon of the *Queen Elizabeth*, where the menu in peacetime would have offered a choice of twenty delicious dishes for breakfast, and here we were with one extremely small, boiled egg and two, thin slices of greyish-coloured bread. I heard, a long time afterwards, that provisioning troop ships was a big racket in those days and those concerned were feathering their nests as fast as they could. It was us who had to suffer.

The *Q.E.* was one of the few ships which did not sail in convoy. I think this was because she had a very good turn of speed, but that didn't make for a rapid journey. She steered a zig-zag course in an attempt to avoid detection by u-boats, making a turn every few minutes and on top of that she made a great detour. We had no idea where we were but after a few days it became noticeably warmer and then progressively colder and at the end of a week word went round that the Ambrose Light had been sighted, so our journey was almost at an end as we steamed into New York Harbour.

Within a few hours we, were sailing slowly up the Hudson to the *Q.E.*'s usual berth at Pier 90, gazing at the New York skyline and the Statue of Liberty. We were promptly disembarked into a ferry which took us across to Pennsylvania Station and from there we travelled to Monkton in New Brunswick.

I was very concerned to find that this transit camp was in the grip of a great epidemic of scarlet fever. Each time a new case arose, person in the bed on either side were moved to a quarantine block. So, even if you didn't become ill yourself, there was a good chance of being delayed and, as we were all anxious to get on with our training, this posed a significant threat.

I resolved to keep fit by being out of doors as much as possible and taking plenty of exercise. This policy backfired badly when I broke an ankle playing baseball and there I was in the dreaded hospital for a lengthy spell. The only comfort I could find was that I was on a surgical ward but even there I felt like a sitting target for any stray germs from one of the crowded fever wards.

In the next bed, on one side of me, was a Canadian seaman from a torpedoed oil-tanker. I don't quite know how he came to be in a Royal Canadian Air Force Hospital. On the other side, there lay a very dejected R.A.F. lad who had some kind of sinus problem. He had been within days of completing his pilot training when he suffered temporary loss of sight while coming in to land. He was lucky to survive that.

While I was still in the hospital, the pilot of an Anson which crashed into a hill was brought in. All the others on the aircraft had been killed. I think they were navigation students. Anyway, this pilot was put in a bed near the door and he was repeatedly wheeled off to the operating theatre. I scooted past him in my wheel chair once or twice and the only bits of skin that you could see in the gaps between his bandages were criss-crossed with stitches. He was quite a mess. I had the impression that things weren't going very well for him and we all had to keep absolutely quiet around him. Then one morning, when we awoke, he just wasn't there.

Occasionally, on the radio, we heard news of the air raids at home and this brought my frustration to an absolute peak of torment. I just wanted to get on with my training so that I could get at these people who were dropping bombs on England.

It didn't seem right to be in a place where there was no blackout, no wailing siren and little sign of war. This unrest was with me all the time I was in Canada but, at least I didn't get scarlet fever. After a few weeks of frustration, I was on my way again, albeit with certain restrictions such as avoiding drill and P.T.

Elementary flying training for me took place at De Winton in prairies of Alberta; in fact, while we were there, we took part in the Calgary Stampede Parade. The tempo of work was fairly gentle. We flew Fairchild

One of the Fairchild Cornells that Angus flew at No.1 Elementary Flying Training School, at De Winton, whilst on Course No.82. (*John Gadd Collection*)

Cornells which posed no real problems; in fact they just about landed themselves provided you didn't interfere too much and, being summer, we had no difficulty with the weather. However, it was always better if you could fly very early in the morning when the air was perfectly still. Several times I saw the sun rise while I was airborne and saw it rise again after I had landed.

Altogether, life at De Winton was pretty good. We could depend on regular off-duty times and I used to go to a ranch and hire a horse to ride through the brown and treeless prairie. Little goffers popped up from their holes in the ground and gazed round. There were said to be rattle snakes there too, but I never saw one. A favourite pastime for a Saturday afternoon was to visit Eaton Department Store in Calgary to choose things as gifts to send home.

Away to the west – at a distance of about 80 miles – the monotonous flatness of the prairie gave way to the Rocky Mountains. At the end of the course my instructor treated me to a marvellous experience. He flew

Fairchild Cornells pictured at No.1 Elementary Flying Training School, De Winton. The Cornell was a single-engine two-seater trainer that was powered by a 200hp engine. (*John Gadd Collection*)

us across to the Rockies. It was purely a joy ride; I merely had to sit and revel in the scenery and the flying, both of which were tremendous. We didn't just fly over and look down. That would have been good enough, but we did better. My instructor flew us in great, breath-taking swoops, down into the valleys, twisting and turning then up and along the peaks in fast, contour-hugging, aerial gallops. Above certain limits, such thrills always makes me laugh. My capacity for excitement explodes into a kind of delirium of joy. I sat there revelling in this most crazy of flying experiences, gasping as we plunged down from the top of the mountain and seemed to fall headlong into the valleys, thousands of feet below. The scenery was absolutely spectacular and this was a fantastic, exhilarating way to enjoy it.

I moved on to 34 Service Flying Training School at Medicine Halso in Alberta, a place with a reputation for being the coldest spot in Canada, but there was far too much to think about to notice the weather. Here, there was an entirely different atmosphere. We were about to lose our boyish, care-free innocence. Everything about the place had a bleak, unforgiving look to it. People always seemed to be in a hurry with preoccupied expressions on their faces. The instructors were not the cheerful, relaxed type we had known at De Winton. From the moment we arrived, it was clear we were in for a hard time. In a sense this was R.A.F. training at its best: if you survived this you would survive anything.

We assembled in a lecture-room for the opening address. There we were told, 'There are forty-two of you in this room now. At the end of the course there will be twenty-eight. Seven of you will be eliminated for failing to reach the necessary flying standard, six of you for failing ground school subjects and one of you will be dead.'

I glanced at my fellow trainees as we left the room. I was wondering which one of us was going to die. They all looked very full of life. I caught sight of my reflection in a glass-panelled door and I realised that I was as liable as anyone to succumb to any of the pitfalls that had just been coldly listed. With a mental shrug I said to myself, 'You may not be able to argue with statistics, but you can make it damn difficult for them to catch you.'

No.34 Service Flying Training School held the efficiency penant, an uninspiring plain white flag that flew from the masthead on the parade ground. It was also the International Service School: we had Belgian, Dutch, Free French and Norwegians there yet, apart from a pleasant ex-Belgian cavalry colonel, there was no sense of Allied solidarity. Some of the Norwegians were actually hostile. I had a confrontation with one of them, a man who had killed German soldiers with his bare hands and then rowed himself across the North Sea in an open boat. Trust me to get involved with this one.

The celebrations of the Norwegians when they had completed the course were dreaded. Armed guards had been called in several times and, from their base on an island in Lake Ontario, the Norwegian Air Force terrorised the people of Toronto who couldn't go out at night in safety. I was greatly puzzled by the uncivilised nature of these young men, but it didn't put me off Norwegians. Every country is capable of producing people like that.

I was lucky at Medicine Hat in having an agreeable instructor who was also a first-class pilot, although at that time he hadn't much experience as an instructor. Some chaps were unfortunate in having bad tempered instructors. Several times I saw trainee pilots walking away from the aircraft in tears. One of these had been a policeman in Liverpool's Dockland, so he wasn't soft, but everything had to be completed to perfection.

We were flying Harvards – excellent training aircraft, not too easy to fly so they produced capable pilots, and that is what this training station set out to do. The ground instructors worked well in excess of normal syllabus requirements in that they were available after duty hours at night when we were free to go for extra instruction. They had also devised ingenious, synthetic, training devices. One of these was years ahead of its time. A link-trainer without its top was positioned in a large, darkened room. Suddenly a light shone on a model of an enemy aircraft suspended from the ceiling. Immediately you swung the link-machine round, calling out at the same time your assessment of the situation, 'ME110. 400 yards, angle of 30, deflection 1½, fire.' Then you pressed the button and, if your calculation had been correct, a bell rang and a light went out.

The whole place was geared up for training efficiency; nobody relaxed for a moment. I don't recall ever having a bad time at Medicine Hat. You certainly never relaxed in the air. You had to concentration on flying exercises under the constant vigilance of the instructor who roamed the sky in a distinctly-marked Harvard. He tried to sneak up and get on your tail; you waggled your wings to show you had seen him and away he'd go, looking for another victim. If he managed to get on the tail of a solo student, he'd report him to his Flight Commander. What followed would be a dressing down that would reduce the poor lad to the lowest levels of misery. Sometimes you would hear the closing comments of just such a

Angus Findon's flying brevet, awarded at the end of his flying training. (John Gadd *Collection*)

conversation, with the Flight Commander's voice bellowing, 'Two weeks – two weeks at the very most and you'll be bloody dead, back in England. Now get out!'

At the end of this course, getting our 'wings' was just a weary formality – no celebration, no party – but now, at least, things became a little more peaceful. I sat on my bunk and sewed the wings and sergeant's stripes onto my two tunics and my battledress top, then wrote home to say I had made it.

As predicted, there were fourteen who hadn't. I had nearly made it fifteen. On one sortie, flying solo, things had started to go wrong. There was a stiff cross-wind; in peace-time training a student wouldn't have been allowed to fly solo in such conditions. I almost managed to land but the aircraft swung and hit a flare. I smoothed out the swing with a burst of power and tried again but now I came down on top of the next flare and knocked it to bits. I decided to open-up and go around again but in doing so I hit most of the remaining flares and put the whole flare path out of action. A red Verey light sailed up from the control tower and, soon after this, I saw the illuminated landing light being swung round, indicating a change of runway – thank God for that. This took some little time and the sky over Medicine Hat soon became crowded with aircraft returning from cross-country flights joining those on circuit work.

A solo cross-country student, one of the foreign ones, made an odd mistake at this point. Seeing no runway lighting, he flew on for a few minutes and saw a row of lights coming up ahead that seemed good enough. He lowered his undercarriage and proceeded to land – right up the main street of a nearby town. It was decent of them to have a street pointing into wind. I, meanwhile, was becoming increasingly concerned about the prospect of fitting myself into what would obviously be a very busy circuit pattern, particularly as I did not want to cut out an impatient instructor, and there were always plenty of those.

But it wasn't at all easy to locate the other aircraft. They didn't have flashing lights all over them like aeroplanes do now and if, for example, you were right behind one, you just saw the white tail-light and you had to look very carefully to be sure it wasn't a star or a distant light on the ground.

I was stooging around, doing my best, but feeling rather overstretched by these events. Suddenly, I was horribly startled by a great burst of noise and a light raced across the sky just above me. Now you can fly a noisy Harvard so close to another that the wing tips touch, but you won't hear its engine. On that basis I think this one was just a few feet above me. It gave me such a fright that my mouth went as dry as dust and a bit of gum I was chewing stuck uncomfortably to my tongue.

Eventually, we were all strung out for landing and a new flare-path was ready. A green Verey light curved through the air in front of the control tower: we were cleared to land. I was at the start of the downwind leg at that moment. There was one aircraft ahead of me and I watched the red and green of his navigation lights as he turned onto his final approach. He came down to a few hundred feet above ground and then he ground-sheered off and climbed away: he didn't seem to like it. I had been doing my downwind vital actions and I now tapped out my identification letter. Back it came to me from a green Aldis lamp – my turn for landing. As I straightened up on the final approach, I noticed the flare-path seemed to be moving sideways, cross wind again, even worse than before. I checked the drift with rudder, then more rudder but still the flare path was slipping away sideways and so I pushed on even more rudder. I noticed I was too high, so I closed the throttle completely. 'Damn all wind gradient here,' I thought, 'it's all going sideways.'

Then a lot of horrible things happened in very quick succession. The aircraft shuddered, a wing dropped, and the ghastly realisation of what was now happening came to me. I took recovery action, but it was too late. I was falling out of the sky, spinning. I sat there, helpless, shouting, 'No! No!' Spinning in on the approach was such a well-known danger and I had dropped right into the trap. I remembered to knock the magneto switches to the 'off' position. As the aircraft hit the ground, there was a tremendous jolt and a shower of sparks came up as a wing tip dug into the runway. The whole thing cartwheeled and there was a great screeching noise and a sort of scream as a tyre was ripped off and the aircraft twizzled round. The cockpit filled with smoke: there were thumps, crashes, screeches – ghastly cacophony of awful, destructive noises. And then it all came to a standstill, beautifully quiet and the cold night air swept in and pushed the smoke out of the cockpit.

There was no sense of relief at being alive, just the dreadful feeling that now my flying days must be over. Headlights came speeding down the runway and the wailing siren of the crash-tender grew louder. The crew leap out in their asbestos suits and the ambulance stopped nearby. Its rear doors opened and a stretcher popped out with admirable speed.

I roused myself and climbed out of the wreckage. Amazingly, I wasn't hurt. The straps had dug in and bruised my shoulders a bit, but the aircraft looked an awful mess. I remember feeling for one dreadful moment that I was going to cry. I asked if I could ride back on the crash-tender and they let me do that. I enjoyed the ride, not least because I could feel the solid weight of the vehicle, with its large wheels firmly on the ground. It contrasted well with the way things had been over the previous half-hour.

The next morning, I was on the mat in front of the Chief Flying Instructor. I was amazed to find him smiling. 'You were very lucky last night Findon,' he said. 'Reading the accident report, I am only surprised we are not arranging a funeral for you. Spinning in from 200 feet usually has a permanent effect on people.' He then went on to teach me more about cross-wind landing techniques and the pitfalls of these conditions. Very decently, the endorsement he made in my logbook merely said, 'Heavy landing. Night.'

Curiously, nobody swore at me for the enormous delays I had caused, first by knocking out the flare-path, then by blocking the runway with a

A North American Harvard of No.1 Flying Instructor School at Trenton, Ontario, Canada. (*John Gadd Collection*)

pranged Harvard. Possibly my good luck had dumbfounded them. It was the following night that Medicine Hat got its statistics in order. One of our chaps was killed, the only married one among us and that seemed to make it worse.

We had a few weeks leave at the end of the course and this came welcome rest. Being winter, there wasn't a lot to do. I enjoyed a fair amount of skating. Mainly, though, the impetus seemed to have gone out of life and I was feeling depressed. Pneumonia and a broken ankle had cost me a lot of time but now I was posted to the Royal Canadian Air Force Station at Trenton for the Flying Instructor Course. For me the war had been put on hold. I felt I might just as well have been a civilian. I could never have guessed at the time that this would become a short cut to an operational squadron.

A Canadian on the course, Flight Lieutenant Bill Brady, had done two operational trips in England and when we went flying, I liked to hear of his time with fighter squadrons. We would sit in the corner of the crew-room with a bottle of Coke or a doughnut and I would ask Bill about fighter tactics – though it seemed I wasn't going to have much need for such information. My instructor, K. Perado, was also a wonderful man – very strict in the cockpit but full of fun. I did my best to let myself be turned into a good flying instructor, but I told him frankly how disappointed I was. I didn't think there was any escape, yet Perado had a twinkle in his eye when he said, 'Leave that to me.'

One day, at the end of the course, he came to the crew room, stood in the doorway and called out, 'Slim! Come here!' He gave me a playful punch on the shoulder and said, 'You're going back to Blighty fellow. Listen, if you can't get on Spitfires get Mustangs. You'll like them – and give those Germans hell, remember that.'

A huge wave of gratitude came over me as powerful as it had when the selection board had said, 'We think you'll make a pilot.' I was back on course. Perado was one of the many fine men I met in my Air Force days. I believe he got back on operational work flying Liberators. I hope he survived. He had tremendous leadership qualities; the world needs men like him. I am a firm believer in the theory that many of our present-day problems are due to the loss of vast numbers of such people in two world wars and several smaller ones.

A view of the airfield at Trenton taken from the cockpit of a Harvard during Angus' time at No.1 Flying Instructor School. (*John Gadd Collection*)

So then it was back to Monkton, the transit camp, to wait for a boat. Two of us used to go for long walks to while away the monotonous days of waiting. One afternoon, we were conscious of a curious rushing sound – something big and heavy hurrying along. We stared around the flat white countryside then up at the sky. Nothing. Then my companion laid down and pressed an ear against the snow. He jumped up quickly and pointing down he said, 'Bloody hell, Fin! It's underneath us. We're on top of the river and this lot must be thawing.

Lets go.' As we hurried away, I remembered how, from the air, you could see movement of water under the ice as a great expanse of water just south of Trenton began to freeze up and how Perado had scared me a bit by lowering the undercarriage of the Harvard and banging the wheels down hard against the great sheet of ice, so that it cracked. He then worked along three lines and at last a huge triangle of ice several, acres in area, slurped up and shattered in thousands of pieces. Perado had glanced over his shoulder and grinned at my startled expression.

Chapter 3

Burma

At last we left Monkton. We sailed from Halifax aboard the *Louis Pasteur*, another fast, unescorted vessel, much smaller than the *QE*. It was a crowded ship as they all were on the UK run in 1944. Lying in my hammock at night, I found I could touch, using hands and feet, eleven other hammocks.

There was a bit of leave back in England but apart from seeing my mother (my father had died while I was at Medicine Hat) I didn't want leave; I just wanted to be with aeroplanes and get on with the job. Also, I felt uncomfortable. I had learnt not to ask for news of my old friends: so many of them now were dead. I tried to avoid being seen by their parents because it seemed a bit selfish of me to be alive.

My next stop was Whitley Bay for a Commando course which I thought was rather irrelevant. The second-front started while we were there, the Normandy invasion, and we used to listen to its progress on the BBC news. We paid particular attention when the announcer reached the part with details of R.A.F. losses when, for instance, he might say, 'From these and other operations, eighteen of our aircraft failed to return,' and we would glance at each other, all with the same thought – eighteen places closer to a job on a squadron.

It was becoming very clear that the R.A.F. had far more aircrew than it was likely to need. One day, we were all on parade when the order came, 'Fall out all QFI's. Remainder, stand fast.' Just three of us left the ranks and went up to the N.C.O. in charge. I thought to myself, 'Well, for heaven's sake, what do they want three qualified flying instructors for now?' But it wasn't that. We were given travel warrants and told we had been posted to an advanced flying unit at Peterborough. Also, we were treated like V.I.P.s. Instead of the usual three-tonner to take us to the station, a staff car arrived driven by a smart, uniformed girl and she took us there in style. My instructor rating had at last paid off.

The object of the Peterborough Course was to familiarise us with U.K. flying conditions, the use of radio aids and night navigation. It was much easier to find your way around at night than by day. A plentiful supply of beacons flashing their identification letter made it simple.

But we had seven fatal accidents while we were there. I think the reason for that was that although we were all qualified pilots, we were relatively inexperienced and had a certain amount of freedom that gave us plenty of opportunity for breaking our necks. At a nearby American base, where Lockheed P-38 Lightnings were making many sorties each day over enemy territory, in the same period of time they had no losses at all.

There was great excitement at Peterborough when our postings eventually came through, though individual reactions varied greatly. One of the chaps had seen the list in the orderly room but he didn't look too happy.

'Where are we going?' I asked.

He stared at me for a moment, shook his head slowly before saying, 'Bloody Jungle Airforce. Far East. Oh my God.'

It came as a bit of a surprise to me too. I had never thought of that remote, little war in Burma where there were no pubs or dances, probably no beer either – but I didn't want to be unhappy.

'At least it's a job,' I said.

'You're welcome,' he replied. 'All grinning little Japs waiting to torture you and horrible tropical diseases, not to mention snakes and scorpions. No thanks. Not me.'

Our Australian companions made their contribution, 'You don't have to worry about the Japs, whacker, the climate will kill you. You'll go all green and just rot away. We're going to Italy.'

Some of the people on the Far East assignment tried to get out of the posting. One chap had an uncle in the Air Ministry and this very senior officer had to leap out of a hot bath to deal with his nephew's urgent phone call. Without any effort at all, though, I was offered an escape route. I was told I had to report to the station adjutant.

This was the one and only time in my Air Force days that I had a link with civilian life. I didn't want my service and home backgrounds to become mixed up. The fact that my family and the adjutant's family knew each other probably had something to do with my being sent for. I sensed that the adjutant was not happy about this meeting either. He nodded at me when I went in, saluted and made a show of fiddling about with some papers on his desk.

Then he cleared his throat and spoke carefully, 'Well now, Findon. You've enjoyed your time here I hope. Found it useful?'

'Thank you, sir. Yes.'

'Mmm, good, good. I was sorry to hear you had lost your father recently.' There was a long pause. 'That leaves your mother all alone, doesn't it?'

I nodded and said quietly, 'Yes, sir.'

'You know Findon, this war is very nearly over now, thank God. I expect she is looking forward to seeing you at home, don't you think?'

I made a weak attempt at evading the issue, 'Yes, sir. I shall be home tomorrow, sir.'

'That's not what I meant,' said the adjutant gruffly. 'You will be home on embarkation leave. How do you think your mother will feel about that?'

'She wouldn't want me to dodge it, sir.'

The adjutant rubbed his chin thoughtfully, 'Mmm, I see.' He got up, walked to the door, opened it and he smiled at me, 'Good luck, Findon,' he said. I thanked him and saluted then shook the hand that was held out to me as I left his office.

Just before we left Peterborough, half a dozen of us had our noses rubbed in the sombre side of war. We were detailed to represent the R.A.F. and act as pall-bearers. A damaged Lancaster had crashed into a hangar on landing and, among the casualties, was the flight engineer. He had been returned to his family for burial.

We shined our boots, polished our buttons and got into the back of a three-ton truck. This took us to a small, terraced house in a narrow street. All the curtains were drawn and up and down the road slight movements revealed neighbours at their windows as we clattered out of the lorry in our heavy drill boots. We were shown into a little room where we sat in suffocating silence, apart from the ticking of a clock. The phrase 'ill at ease' kept going through my mind; we were very ill at ease. There was a framed photograph of a flight sergeant and a girl in a wedding dress, which I think we all caught sight of and looked away quickly. It seemed a long while before one of the undertaker's men poked his head round the door and said, 'This way gents.'

We followed him down the narrow hall and into a bedroom. It seemed repugnant to be so close to a coffin. In a moment we were going to lift it and the whole thing filled me with horror. There was a double bed in the room which had just a white sheet and a pillow on it. The pillow had a hollow in its middle and down the sheet were flower petals and the outline of a human body.

We stooped to get our shoulders under the coffin. I think the weight surprised us all – I heard one or two slight gasps. We tried to carry it as smoothly and respectfully as possible. I couldn't help thinking that the weight on my shoulders was the weight of a fellow airman – dead. Christ, this was horrible.

The coffin was slid into the hearse and we got back into our three-tonner, going down to the far end and discreetly lighting smokes. Nobody said anything. What could anyone say? We were shaken. At the cemetery the coffin was wheeled along on a kind of trolley. We stepped up to the grave one-by-one and saluted. Many times since, I have had to do this and I always noticed the reproachful glances you got from the civilian mourners. What were they thinking? Perhaps they were asking, 'Why couldn't it have been one of us in that box?'

The chap's poor wife stood staring down at the coffin. She gave a pitiful cry and slumped toward the open grave. Two of the undertaker's men grabbed her before she could fall in. I drank a lot of beer that night and for once I didn't listen to the news. If I had, I would have wanted the announcer to say, 'All our aircraft returned safely.'

I found it very hard on leaving England. On my embarkation leave, I walked alone for hours over the downland I loved so much, fixing views in my mind and feeling the springy turf beneath my feet.

The portside of the ship, as we sailed away from Liverpool, was noticeably empty during the first few hours of the voyage. I think a lot of people had a premature homesickness. The sight of England fading away in the distance was deeply and painfully moving. But we soon bounced back and began to take an interest in the voyage. This troop-ship was the *Alcantara* and, apart from the usual dreadful food, it was a pleasent voyage with enjoyable duties. We manned the Oerlikon gun-turrets, high over the ship's sides, though all our watches were uneventful: the Germans hadn't any aircraft to spare to attack us.

We disembarked, after several days, in Alexandria and from there to Cairo the journey was pretty slow but interesting. Our Australian friends appeared to have quite a bit of local knowledge and we often heard them, as we got closer to Cairo, shouting what we took to be greetings in the native tongue. We quickly caught on and added our voices. The civilians on the platform included many smartly-dressed men and women – a cosmopolitan selection as one might expect around a big city – but they didn't appear to be impressed. Stony-faced, they ignored this lusty goodwill and well they might. I found out later, to my deep shame, that the things we had been yelling so enthusiastically were Arab obscenities of the most intimate and offensive variety. Even now I can very nearly blush when I think of our outrageous indecency.

We hadn't long to wait in Cairo before we were posted to, the Operational Training Unit (O.T.U.) that most coveted course of any pilot's career and we arrived in the Canal Zone at 73 O.T.U.

As soon as possible after arrival, I went to one of the hangars because a decision had to be made. We were free to express a preference for the type of aircraft we would train on. In the hangar were Spitfires, Thunderbolts, and Kittyhawks. The Kittyhawks were reserved for the Australians who would go on to Mustang squadrons in Italy. It's a sad fact that all the Australians, who were at Peterborough with us, and then again at Fayid, were to be dead within a few months. They came up against the German light, anti-aircraft units which proved fatal.

The choice, then, lay between Spitfires and Thunderbolts. I had never been near either and now I was walking among them, marvelling at the sleek beauty of the Spitfire and the huge, though wonderfully streamlined bulk of the Thunderbolt.

You could easily look into the Spitfire cockpit as you stood beside it, but the Thunderbolt? I was puzzled to wonder how a pilot even got into one of these things. You could almost stand upright under its wingtip. I didn't know then that the spring-loaded flaps on the sides and belly of the fuselage perfectly blended into the metal skin. These provided hand grips and toe-holds and, when you got used to their position, you shinned up the side and onto the wing route in a flash. But now I dragged a trestle up and stood on that. A glance into the cockpit instantly revealed the truth of a saying I had heard that, 'The British build the pilot around the plane. The Americans build the plane around the pilot.'

The spacious cockpit had the seductive luxury of a limousine. Quite apart from that, I was amazed at what I saw. Many of the instruments were familiar, of course, but the throttle quadrant had four levers on it instead of two, and the levers themselves had switches built into them.

This aircraft was obviously a whole new experience. There were levers, switches, knobs, buttons and gauges; the whole effect was fascinating. It looked like a flying cinema organ. At least you would never be bored. But it was very difficult to decide.

Imagine being in a car showroom. There is a Lamborghini there and a Rolls-Royce. You can have either – for free. I couldn't resist taking another look at the Spitfire. The desire to fly it ached in my head. To fly that aircraft, which is now a legend, was probably the ambition of every single-engine pilot. How could one resist such an opportunity?

But what of the future? Spitfire pilots had been coming off the supply line for quite a while. I would find myself queuing up for a squadron. Thunderbolt pilots were a rare bread by comparison; they possibly numbered only a few hundred. I stood gazing up at the Thunderbolt and feeling uneasy. I knew nothing of this aircraft except that it had been designed as a long-range fighter for the protection of American heavy bombers. I smiled at myself, remembering an American pilot I had heard in a pub in England who said, 'Yes, sir. I fly the P-47.' I also heard a rumour that this aeroplane could exceed the speed of sound in a dive. At that time it was as much a mystery to me as the war in Burma. All I had heard of that were joking references to the green hell.

How did the Thunderbolt fit into all this – a little-known aircraft in a little-known war? I had no idea. However, the important thing was to get into action with a squadron as quickly as possible. So I chose the Thunderbolt.

Apart from the gratifying knowledge that becoming an operational pilot was now a reality, the prospect of flying the Thunderbolt was tremendously exciting. Remembering how one of these from an American base had loomed up on me when I was a bit lost ealier that year in England and how, on my embarkation leave, I had seen one over the South Downs, the thought of flying a Thunderbolt myself was exhilarating in the extreme.

Our official welcome to Fayid by the Station Commander, a very successful fighter pilot in the early days of the Burma Campaign, suffered an unexpected delay. A Thunderbolt had only just crashed, shortly after take-off, killing the pilot. Group Captain Kerry had made an immediate preliminary investigation. He then came straight to see us and gave a very upbeat talk about the work that lay ahead of us. There was no trace of the ponderous gloom that so often hung over a peacetime station after a fatal accident. Not that we dismissed these things from our minds. We always wanted to know the cause of the crash because we wanted to learn about the sort of mistakes that could happen and make sure that we didn't repeat them.

The crash at Fayid was the kind that would be put down to pilot error, qualified with the remark, 'Inexperience on type'. Nobody liked to be noticeably slow in joining a formation after take-off. Unfortunately, this pilot pulled his aircraft round too hard and began turning before he had built up adequate speed. The Thunderbolt was very fussy in this respect and completely unforgiving. It would flick unless you had a lot of sky under you. It was as simple as that.

I have to spend a few paragraphs dealing with specific aspects of the Thunderbolt so I think I may as well use the name that we used to refer to them, the abbreviated form, T'Bolt. This is how they will be referred to in the rest of this story.

The first thing we had to do with the T'Bolt was to learn about everything in the cockpit. There would be a written examination on fuel, the hydraulic systems and various other aspects of its operation. On top of this, you had to memorise exactly the position of about forty different items: instruments, levers, switches and buttons. Then you sat in the cockpit and a thick bandage was tied over your eyes. The examiner stood on the wing root and in rapid time called out the names of these forty items. Fuel booster pump, fuel pressure gauge, tail wheel lock, main switch, oxygen control, normal, emergency, aileron trim, bomb fuse panel, landing light, radiator cooler shutter switch and so on. You had to put the tip of one finger precisely on the thing he named. No hesitating and no fumbling.

Up to that time, all of the aircraft we had flown were dual control trainers so, if something went wrong, the instructor could take over. The Thunderbolt was a single-seater. An instructor stood on the wing root as you taxied out on your first solo; as much as anything, this was to help to avoid taxying accidents. All single-engine, tail-wheel aircraft gave the pilot very little visibility straight ahead so you zig-zagged along to avoid hitting any ground markers or other aircraft. With the T'bolt, there was more aeroplane stretching out in front of the cockpit than any of us had yet seen. For the first few minutes of your first solo, you had the comforting presence of an instructor riding on the wing. You lined up on the runway, performed your pre-take-off vital action drill – making a special point of pulling the tail wheel lock – and then the instructor patted you on the back and climbed down. You were now very alone.

You looked across at the black and white chequered caravan parked clear of the runway on your right and there you saw the top half of the airfield controller in his glass-roofed box. He picked up his green Aldis lamp and pointed it at you. There it was, a steady green light coming straight at you. So, lick your lips and push the throttle over. Most aircraft showed a kind of impatience to get in the air, once flying speed had been reached – but not the T'Bolt. You could get the tail up fairly soon but then it just roared on, easily using a mile of runway. At 120 m.p.h. you made a definite backward movement of the stick and lifted it off. The wheels retracted promptly and the cockpit canopy slid over your head at the touch of a switch. That a bit of the American luxury treatment there.

The things you were to do on that first flight had all been carefully explained. Allowances had been made for the fact that the power and speed could take your breath away. The first solo took two hours from start to finish and it was, indeed, a remarkable flying experience.

The first landing was also a bit sensational due to the high approach speed – twice as fast as anything we had yet flown. There was a separate landing ground a few miles from Fayid used for this and an instructor was in radio contact, talking you down. If your speed fell off a bit, he was on to you immediately. Without him, some first landings might have been far more spectacular and very expensive. The cost of a T'Bolt was £17,000 – the price of three Spitfires.

Every aspect of the work at Fayid was thoroughly enjoyable. I liked the dive-bombing practice, despite disliking the bomb itself as a weapon. I had a chance to watch this exercise from the ground one day in one of the plotting huts on the range.

The dive commenced at 8,000 feet and the bomb was released at 3,000 feet. The remarkable thing about this was that, until the bomb

This is almost certainly the first Thunderbolt that Angus flew solo, KJ136, whilst at No.27 Operational Training Unit, RAF Fayid, Egypt. The flight, on 29 November 1944, lasted two hours. (*John Gadd Collection*)

burst, the whole process was almost invisible. You might occasionally catch sight of the T' Bolt as it windowed for its dive, then it vanished. The distant whine of the engine rose then fell as the aircraft rounded out and the constant speed unit changed the pitch of the propeller blades. At that moment, a cloud of smoke billowed up from the target area and you might just again catch sight of the T'Bolt scudding away in the distance, weaving to try and make itself a difficult target.

Whether or not the target was hit depended largely on the pilot's ability to judge a 12 degrees angle with complete accuracy. We had no special bomb sight. We used the quite ordinary and very effective reflector gunsight. It was the only bit of British equipment in the T'Bolt, and a fine piece of precision equipment it was. Holding the bright red dot of the gunsight on the target, a quick glance at the altimeter, 3,000 feet coming up, pull back 12 degrees and as you did so the target disappeared under the nose of the aircraft. At 12 degrees precisely, you press the button. Now weave and twist as you pull away and make yourself an impossible target for the light Ack-Ack, or sweep up in a wide, climbing turn to position for another attack, glancing over your shoulder to see where your bomb landed.

The T'Bolt was beautifully steady in the dive, in fact it must have been the most perfect dive-bombing aircraft. One afternoon, at the end of our working day, we were gathered for the assessment session to hear the results of our bombing and firing practice. I got a shock when my score was read out and the instructor remarked that it was about the worst we had ever had. 'You have to do better than that, Findon.' Now I knew I had scored a good 80% direct hits and the remainder pretty close. There must have been a mistake. I smiled to myself and thought tomorrow I would get a 100% correct. That would show them.

Then he said, 'Well here's a good one, Sergeant Jones.' (His name wasn't Jones. I don't want to embarrass the man.) '80% direct hits.' I glanced at this Sergeant Jones, whose face was going very red. Compliments were showered on him all round and I began to feel rather sorry for him. The next day the error had been detected and an announcement was made. I rather wish that it hadn't been found out – I would have liked poor Jones to have had that bit of a boost. He was very depressed and his results were again dreadful.

Quite apart from failing to damage the enemy, reasonable accuracy was vital because the Army would often call for a strike just ahead of its own positions and at the rate Sergeant Jones was going, he'd be doing the Japs work for them. I had a quiet chat with him and tried to give him some useful advice.

I must say that I had a great advantage over my fellow pilots. There had been dive-bombing practice at the instructor school in Canada and in general terms, the flying at Peterborough had added to my experience. These chaps had come straight from their service schools in Rhodesia. My turn for a discomforting experience was yet to come!

I was signing up for an aerobatic flight which I had just completed. The flight commander stood nearby and he asked me, 'What speed do you use for a loop?'

There was only one answer, '360, sir'.

He shook his head, 'Anybody can do the T'Bolt at that speed. You want to work your speed down until you are really flying the aeroplane. Then there's something to it.' It was a dangerous piece of advice but innocently I accepted it. After all, I wanted to be as capable a pilot as possible.

My next trip was an oxygen climb to 40,000 feet, though I went to 42,000 just to be sure I had made it. I had a lot of height so why not use it for a good aerobatic session? I descended a little first but the sky seemed dark and lonely at that height and the ground was featureless, just a great, brown stain beneath me.

I performed some horizontal aerobatics: barrel rolls and slow rolls, with maximum rate turns to get the feel of the point where control would be lost. Below 30,000 feet I began manoeuvres in the vertical plain: upward rolls, rolls off the top of a loop, loops at increasingly lower speeds – 350, 340, 330, 320, 300 – Oh God! What's this? She wasn't going to get over the top.

The T'Bolt wallowed on its back. The nose began to swing and there it was. All through our training, we had been warned about the inverted spin – the spin from which recovery was just about impossible. Even normal spins were prohibited in aircraft over 3 tons. I gave it hard, opposite rudder and pulled the stick back to stop the nose moving down. This simplified things so that I was now in an inverted dive. The turning had stopped. The aircraft was accelerating very rapidly and I glanced at the instrument panel – but it didn't make sense. I had never seen an altimeter unwinding so fast and the airspeed indicator was swinging round pretty wildly too. The needle on the vertical speed indicator seemed to have completely vanished until I saw it jammed up against its stop. I was pulling hard back on the stick now and the nose seemed to be coming up, just a little, then the aircraft jolted and went on diving. I put two hands on the stick and pulled – nothing happened except more jolting and shaking so I decided to get out.

The pin came out of my safety harness alright and I drew my feet back ready to push myself up as soon as the canopy was ejected. When I tried to lean forward, I found I couldn't move: the acceleration was just too great. There were lots of little notices inside the T'Bolt all nicely printed on metal plates. I caught sight of one printed in red. The large lettering read, 'In a dive increase, never decrease power.' It seemed quite the wrong thing to add power to the situation when we were screaming towards the ground, but I did it. I gave it full throttle. Now my ears began to hurt and I screamed to relieve the pressure. I was shaking my head from side to side to try to stop the pain and I suddenly caught sight of my port wing – or what should have been my port wing ! It was a fascinating sight ; the whole surface was covered in a rippling mass of white paper, just the muzzles of the guns poking out in front. The featureless mass of the desert beneath gave no impression of its rapidly increasing proximity. I continued pulling on the stick with both hands, wondering if it would bend or worse still, break. I saw the altimeter reading off the height down to single figures now. Then there was more bumping, and the nose began to come up. Getting into thicker air, combined with having trimmed the aircraft slightly tail-heavy when I started my vertical aerobatics was now having some effect.

Gradually, the aircraft flattened out and I eased off the power. Off to the right, I could see the Suez Canal. I wondered if my airspeed indicator had been damaged: it seemed stuck on 600 m.p.h. Anyway, it was sheer bliss to be out of that dive although my ears were still hurting. I just sat there in a numbed state and whooshed up the canal then, with the speed down to normal cruising, I turned back to Fayid. The aircraft behaved perfectly and showed no signs of the disturbing things it had been doing just a few minutes previously.

A little while after this, something more serious occurred in the matter of diving T'Bolts. Three of them were having a tail chase. The leader dived and the other two followed. All three of them crashed at high speed into the desert. Then on a dive-bombing flight, one of the T'Bolts got stuck in a dive but the pilot managed to bale out. The Group Captain was heard to remark that, 'The desert round here is getting to look like a bloody dartboard.'

On leaving Fayid we had an unusually comfortable journey, on board a Sunderland Flying Boat. With us were several ENSA people; not actually ENSA but some form of troop-entertainment people. We used to get the worst of them out East and having to have some of them with us was not a good thing at all as they considered themselves top-level showbiz people. They expected the best seats and priority in everything. In addition to

The Christmas Day dinner menu for the personnel at RAF Fayid on 25 December 1944. (*John Gadd Collection*)

this, they would only talk to the officers, which was a merciful release for us.

We arrived in Karachi where I was introduced to curry, and a very hot one! Soon, we were off again on our way to Poona and, in readiness for the Jungle Self-preservation Training School, we were issued with bush hats. Those who had returned from Jungle School were showed us the leather headband inside their hats, darkened with sweat.

'That's what yours will look like if you use them now,' they said.

The journey from Poona in three-ton trucks was a marvellous experience. Jungle School was very well organised, staffed by people who had lived in Burma, including a number who were Burmese hill tribesmen. Tho taught us a tremendous amount about living off the land and personal survival. We learnt Burmese phrases; how to ask for the basics and other useful expressions. We also learned about Burmese etiquette.

For those who were not content with the catapult, there was the Burmese bow, which was made from a piece of bamboo, even the string, and fired a mud pellet. Until you learnt to twist the bow on releasing the string you had a very painful time, as a little ball of hardened mud, which could travel a hundred yards, broke itself to bits on your thumb nail.

You also learnt how to avoid being entertained by the Naga head hunters. The Naga Regiment was part of the Indian Army and a few specimen shrunken heads were available for inspection, together with a necklace of Japanese ears. We were told they wouldn't object to British ears ! We made several treks through the local shrubbery, including sections where Japanese booby traps of every description had been laid and where snipers had concealed themselves in trees. We were expected to spot them, but we never did. Finally, we were divided into groups of four or five, driven a considerable distance from base, and left to make our own way back over the next three days. The grand finale was a climb over a 2,000 foot, miniature mountain known as 'The Saddleback' and after that it was easy going to reach base. The leather band inside our bush hats was very dark by then.

Upon returning to Poona, I found a message instructing me to report to the orderly room and there a corporal said, 'Your commission has come through, sir.' Suddenly, I felt very sad. I had been very happy amongst my sergeant pilot companions and even happier since, a few months ago, I had become a Fight Sergeant. But several of the officers on the course at Fayid had repeatedly urged me to apply for a commission. One of them had said, 'Don't you know it's your duty to seek promotion.' So, I applied and then promptly forgot about it. I didn't expect that an application made in the Middle East would catch up with me in India. I went out and bought myself an officer's cap and the rank markings for my epaulettes and there I was – Pilot Officer Findon.

That evening, I found the Officers' Mess, a very boring, unfriendly place to be in although, of course, it was a transit camp. Transit camps were never very jolly places so I had a drink and went back to my room and began sorting out my clothes. To my great joy, I found that I still had a bush jacket with the three stripes and crown of the Flight Sergeant insignia on the sleeve. An idea came to me. It seemed a rather awful thing to do but I shoved the jacket under my arm, made my way across to the Sergeants' Mess, hid my officer's cap and jacket under a bush and, doing a quick change, I became a Flight Sergeant again. I went in and found my friends who very decently accepted me, even though I was sailing under false colours, and we had a marvellous evening together and I felt a lot better.

Beyond the jungle course, we hoped, lay our squadrons but there was another diversion and, as it turned out, this was quite untypical of any R.A.F. Station. It was a truly murderous place.

This was Yelahanka, about 20 miles north of Bangalore. When we arrived, smoke was billowing from a burning building. We soon found out that there was a pyromaniac on the station and among his targets was the Officers' Mess which, in due course, was burnt down. The flames engulfed the N.C.O.'s quarters which they had to evacuate so rapidly they lost most of their belongings. Only about a third of the fire extinguishers we got hold of were working.

When we reported to the crew room to start flying, we were looked at with a mixture of hostility and contempt. The staff pilots were an unpleasant lot. One of them went outside and shot at a dog and as we heard its cries, they seemed to enjoy our pained expressions. Basically, it seemed they all disliked anybody British. They were a mixture of Canadians and New Zealanders. I had come across this once or twice before. In Montreal, for instance, we had to go about in pairs or run the risk of being dragged down an alley and kicked unconscious.

Things went wrong for me right from the start. I took a T'Bolt up to familiarise myself with the local area. After a while, I saw another T'bolt which appeared to be positioning to get on my tail. I very quickly turned to get the sun in his eyes, reversed the situation and got him in my sights. He flew on steadily so I decided he had had enough and I carried on with my tour. On landing, I was sent for by the C.O. and he lashed into me for undisciplined flying, telling me that, when approached by one of his staff, I had taken violent, evasive action. I suppose his pilot had been upset because I got on his tail ; in effect I had shot him down. In the evening some hard drinking started which went on till well past midnight. Anybody who didn't join in was regarded as stand-offish.

Our N.C.O. aircrew were spared this, though their lives were made miserable in other respects. One of our officers, however, went along with this unhealthy little mob. He was thrown out the back of a truck on the main Bangalore-Yelahanka road and left for dead.

Late one afternoon, I was returning from a long-range, cross – country flight and I thought I would test the accuracy of the homings at Yelahanka. I knew I was right on track and when the bearing I was given agreed with this, that was reassuring. My only criticism was that reception was not very clear. I prepared for landing, pushed my map under my leg so it wouldn't blow around the cockpit when I opened the canopy and reduced height for joining the circuit.

Unknown to me, an aircraft had crashed to the north-west of the base and the C.O. was flying out to look for it. I called up for permission to land and, to my amazement, I was told to fly a heading directly opposite to the one I was on. What had happened was that the

C.O. had called up for a bearing which I wouldn't have heard. All I heard was the bearing which I understood was for me to fly. The sun was low in the sky and in the featureless land around Yelahanka one part looked much like another. I had to assume I had overflown my base.

When I turned, I found my visibility absolutely nil towards the western sky. To navigate, you had to look behind at the ground. I flew on expecting to see the earth yield at any moment. Dawn may come up like thunder in the East, but the night comes down even faster and it was rapidly getting dark. I called for a check bearing and got no answer, the country below was rugged and desolate and far from ideal for a forced landing.

Being lost in an aeroplane is a most miserable experience. In a sense, you become a condemned man: your minutes and numbered and I was well and truly lost. I looked at my map to see if I could orientate on some major feature such as a river. There was none. In that light a railway line or a road wouldn't be visible.

In that part of the world at the time, radio aids were not relied upon. You had to stand or fall by your own navigational ability. I saw a light below me and flew down to see if there was a suitable place for a forced landing. There was a bit of a track that might be alright for a belly-flop and light was coming from a cluster of huts. Circling above, I now climbed, remembering that the higher one flew, the better the chance of radio reception.

I transmitted every 2,000 feet. Above me the stars where coming out; below me the lights I had seen on the ground were disappearing in the gloom. At about 10,000 feet, very faintly, I heard a voice, 'Say again. Receiving you strength 1.'

I called again, throttled back to reduce engine noise and, letting go of the stick, I pressed my earphones against my head. This helped to hear enough to be able to set a heading and gradually the transmissions became clearer. Every five minutes I got a check steer and at last a wonderful sight – there was the flickering row of lights below me and I went down and landed, much relieved.

Nothing was ever said about this incident. A few days later we all went out on a formation practice flying. At 30,000 feet, I was finding it difficult to fly accurately. I was weaving around like a drunk.

'Blue Two, check your oxygen,' I heard someone call. 'Blue Two, I say again, check your oxygen.'

Who the hell was this Blue Two and why wasn't he answering? It suddenly dawned on me that Blue Two was me. I looked at my oxygen gauge. It showed empty. 'Oxygen zero. Returning to base,' I called and I dropped out of formation. This time something was said. 'If you do that on a squadron, you'll get thrown off,' I was told.

What had happened was that as had I closed the cowl gills for take-off, the top of my gauntlet had knocked the oxygen control to the full emergency position. That would empty the whole supply in about 12 minutes.

I was beginning to wonder what mistakes I would make next. Nothing is worse for a pilot than low morale. It seems that one mistake then follows another. My landings were now getting worse and that, in itself, can be terribly depressing.

We ended our time at Yelahanka with something that should have been very enjoyable. An air-show was to be arranged for the benefit of troops stationed in Bangalore. This was probably a form of

V.E. Celebration, the war in Europe having ended a couple of weeks previously.

We flew various formation patterns above the crowd, then moved away while other aircraft came in and did their act. The grand finale was a high-speed Thunderbolt attack on an 'enemy' airfield. The technique here was to level off about two miles from the target and come screeching over at about 500 m.p.h. all guns blazing. I was briefed to fly on the extreme left, passing just in front of the control tower and that was something of a privilege. I thought perhaps the vendetta was at last cooling off. One of the staff pilots was on my right. He looked at me several times during the briefing as if he had something on his mind. The moment arrived and the airfield control called us in. In the background, one could hear the announcement going out over the loudspeaker system, 'Now fix your eyes over to the right for this exciting, etc.' We dived, levelled off and went scudding across the ground. I aimed to pass about 40 feet in front of the control tower which I could now see crowded with spectators. We were just short of the airfield boundary when I caught sight of the man on my right pulling across in front of me. His slipstream hit me and my T'Bolt bucked and swung on its side. The control tower was just a few feet from my wingtip and people ahead of me on the ground were flinging themselves flat.

To this day, I cannot think why anyone would do such a brazenly murderous thing. The slaughter would have been appalling if a T'Bolt had cut through a crowd like that.

I was impatient to land and get hold of the man but he was already out of his cockpit and running across to me as I stopped my engine. He stood there smiling and shaking his head.

'I just can't think what made me do that. I sure am sorry,' he said.

I unclipped my parachute and stood looking at him. A lot of people were watching so this wasn't the time to knock a fellow officer's teeth out.

While travelling from Bangalore to Calcutta, I fell foul of administerative arrangements which hadn't changed since pre-war days and under the provisions was a thing called a Form 4. I was given 400 rupees . This was intended to cover all the needs of an officer in making a rail journey: his ticket, a ticket for his horse, his groom and his personal servant, and meals and fodder for all concerned.

As my ticket cost only 80 rupees and we stopped overnight in Madras, I decided to throw a party there for all my sergeant pilot friends and we had an enormous feast in one of its better hotels. In Calcutta, we were billeted in a small hotel and, on the understanding that this was our last contact with civilisation for a while, we had a party every night. We spent the afternoons in one of the splendid, air-conditioned cinemas and the mornings recovering from the previous night's celebrations. We developed quite a taste for Carooz Gin, an Indian brand that sold quite cheaply, 11 rupees a bottle, and this stuff was known as 'Carooz smooth booze for aircrews'.

We came across a group of bomber chaps who had been twiddling their thumbs out there for some time. A signal had been sent to England calling for four Liberator Airscrews. This had been miss-spelt or miss-read and four Liberator Aircrews had been despatched.

At odd moments, we encountered people who took a morbid interest in telling us how unpleasant we would find things in Burma. There were tales of T"bolts not being able to get airborne and crashing on top of their napalm bombs, going up in flames and how, one time, twelve aircraft went into cloud and only two came out. Such thoughts were pushed aside whilewe waited in expectation of an airlift.

I knew by then that I was going to join No. 34 Squadron . When the movement order came, we waited for transport outside our hotel. It was a long time coming and I wandered down the drive. An old Indian, a Sikh, came up to me and said he would like to tell my fortune. Straight away he squatted in front of me and made some signs in the dust. This seemed like a bit of harmless entertainment so I let him continue. He took hold of one of my hands and gazed it. Then he stood up and with amazing accuracy, told me of a number of events from the past. Then I fell for the obvious temptation – the future. What of that?

'A man called Peters will do something very good for you, sir.' That was all he was prepared to say. I gave him a few rupees and he ambled away.

Then our truck came and we were off. We boarded a Dakota at Dumdum Airport but didn't get far. The weather forced us back to land at Camilla, but at least we were on the way.

Camilla was a desolate place. We lay on the mud floor of a tent all night long, the frogs croaking noisily. However, I any discomfort I speak off was as nothing compared to those endured by the troops in Burma.

Next day, the weather was kinder and the aircraft landed on an airstrip at Kilmagon. I was told I would find my squadron there. I left my kit by the runway and wandered off. A voice hailed me from a small foxhole and I went over to find several people including a Group Captain who was the local commander, 'A cup of char?' he said, and I thanked him. He told me my squadron had moved but he had got a jeep that would take me to meet them a little later. Every now and then, he would gaze about him and then he smiled at me. 'There was a party of Japs reported here earlier,' he said, 'you never know where these blighters are going to pop up since the Army cut off about 20,000 of them when they went through to Rangoon.' Those 20,000 Japs were to be my share of the war as they tried to get through to Malaya or Siam.

On the evening of the day that I joined 34 Squadron, there was a party in the Sergeants' Mess. I was taken along and introduced all round. I forget what we drank; it wasn't beer as that was a great rarity in Burma. I noticed how very basic everything was: our glasses were simply bottles with the tops cut off and the furniture was ammunition boxes. Somebody had just been posted at the end of his tour and I had taken his place in a tent. My companion showed me how to avoid having the soles of my boots chewed up by white ants and other tips such as tying things to tent poles so they wouldn't be washed away when rain came gushing through like a river.

The squadron had only very recently completed its conversion to T'Bolts and one or two of the pilots were still doing familiarisation flights. Remembering the intensity of our training at Fayid, I felt rather

Angus Findon pictured in the cockpit of a Thunderbolt soon after his arrival with 34 Squadron. (*John Gadd Collection*)

concerned for the chaps who had not been quite so intensively trained, though of course they were more experienced as pilots. A few days later, two of them went to practice some dummy strafing, in the course of which one found his engine cutting out.

'Change tanks and switch on your booster pump,' the other said. This was because, for some reason, we used our reserve fuel first then changed to our main tank.

I could imagine this pilot thinking, 'Where the hell is the booster pump?' and he wouldn't have had much time to think, being at low altitude. He failed to restart his engine and he was seen to land heavily in a paddy field. The friend flew over and saw him sitting in the cockpit and assumed he had been knocked out by the impact. The squadron chief went with the medical officer and reached him later that day. He was found, still sitting in the cockpit. But his clothes, his parachute and his service revolver were missing, and his throat had been cut. This was the work of the Burmese roaming bands who killed and plundered their own people, Japs and British alike.

Being a newcomer, I was the natural choice to make the funeral arrangements. It was unusual of course to recover a body. I expect there are many hundreds of wrecked aircraft still with the skeletons of their crews lying in gloomy bits of jungle, General Wingate among them.

There was only one coffin in the store and I had difficulty in persuading the store-keeper to part with it. It was a crude looking thing, all black. I lifted my prize in the back of a jeep and delivered it to the station sick quarters.

Next day, with six N.C.O.s as pall-bearers, we drove to a military cemetery with the coffin on the floor of a 3-ton truck, the rest of us in the squadron's 15cwt truck. The padre appeared and said we would walk the procession to the grave. He added, 'I am glad you have no firing party as I don't like that.'

I unfolded the Union Jack and remembered the strict instructions I had not to let this go into the grave with the coffin. Just then, one of the sergeant pilots came rushing up with a shocked look on his face.

'Fin, the lids fallen off! It wasn't fixed down and – well, there he is just lying there.'

At that moment I saw an airman trudging past carrying a little webbing bag and I called out, 'Airman! What have you got in that bag?'

'Tools, sir,' he said. 'Nothing else?'

'A few nails and things,' he answered.

I confess that I was sheltering behind my rank when I said, 'There is a box up in that lorry. Get up there and nail the lid on.'

The man climbed up and there was a plaintive gasp, 'Sir, you mean this …?'

'That's right. Get on with it.'

The burial then went ahead as planned. I had managed to find a bugler to play the *Last Post* and I took a picture to send to the lad's next of kin. Later, I felt annoyed with myself for the way I had handled the incident with the coffin lid. It shouldn't have happened.

The weather was an ever-present danger and the conditions could change remarkably quickly. That happened all too often. On one occasion, I watched a Spitfire attempting to land. It was raining quite hard and I could just about see the Spitfire groping its way towards the end of the airstrip. I saw it get its wheels down and begin its turn in and

I was thinking how lucky he was to have found somewhere to land. Then his luck didn't hold. The rain suddenly became a deluge and everything was blotted out. The sound of the Merlin engine opening up to power away could just be heard above the noise of the rain. This was a regular occurence.

Our job on 34 Squadron was to provide close support for the Army. Our targets were usually just a little way ahead of the troops and you could see them, perhaps wading through flooded paddy fields towards the village we were just about to attack. They waved to us as we flew over. No risks were too great to help these chaps and we tried extremely hard to battle through the weather to help them out.

Sometimes, after take-off, it was very difficult to join up with the rest of the formation and occasionally an aircraft had to give up, just go back and land, because the formation he was supposed to be part of had vanished into cloud.

Personnel of 34 Squadron pictured with one of its Thunderbolts in August 1945. (*John Gadd Collection*)

Once, we were trying to get through to an important target which had been selected for an earthquake attack ; that was twelve T'bolts in two flights of six. One aircraft was lost on the way out when the pilot's nerve cracked We could hear him jabbering over the R.T. as he went out of control. It was a strange feeling to be so near to him – just a few hundred yards I suppose – but nobody could help. We came out of cloud and found the first flight making a wide turn in front of us. The way ahead was blocked by rising ground and more cloud and suddenly there were too many aircraft and not enough sky. In normal circumstances, a formation leader would increase his speed when making a turn so that the aircraft on the inside was not flying too slowly. In this situation that wasn't possible because we were far too close to the first flight. The order came over the radio, 'Turn individually,' which gave rise to some very odd manoeuvres.

Another time, it seemed that we couldn't even take-off as the airstrip appeared to be sinking. We had already had our briefing ; there was never a met forecast although the weatherman was always present at the debriefing, an Indian officer of very gentle appearance. He would stand at the entrance to the tent and say, 'Please, how has weather been?' and the poor chap would flinch at the short crude replies we gave him. Also, at our briefing no direction-finding radio frequencies were given out as there weren't any and no diversions were given. That's why we often came in with the little yellow light shining on the instrument panel, meaning 15 minutes fuel left.

On the day, we had a water-logged runway. There was urgent need for air support as the Japs had just started their breakthrough at the Sittang Bend. All available senior officers came to look at the airstrip, pressing their heels into it, stamping about trying to decide whether it was safe for the aircraft to take off.

'We'll give it a try,' our C.O. said and we were instructed to use water injection for take-off. This was something we never liked to use because for some reason, immediately after you pressed the button, the engine cut out for a brief instant and, having your engine cut out with a full bomb load under you was rather disturbing to say the least.

We got off all right but the aircraft looked more like a flotilla of speedboats ploughing along the runway, with a great flurry of spray coming up behind them. The weather went from bad to worse all the way and, in the target area, it rain was impenetrable. The minimum altitude for releasing our tail-fused bombs was 300 feet but there was no chance of that – we couldn't even make a strafing run. In fact, conditions were so bad we got mixed up with T'bolts from another squadron and I found myself flying next to one of these. I happened to notice his serial number and I realised it wasn't one of ours.

Angus Findon's officers' pay book. (*John Gadd Collection*)

We hung around for a long time, waiting for a chance to attack, which meant we were going to be very low on fuel. It was much later than usual in the day, due to our delayed take-off and already the light, such as it was, was pretty poor. On our way back to base, the weather was extremely poor with a kind of mist coming up from the ground which merged with the cloud. We turned and worked our way along the iron beam, that is to say the railway line which, in Burma, was an invaluable landmark as there was just the one line running down the middle to Rangoon.

We had heard that an airstrip further south had been cleared of Japs so we headed for that. By this time we all had our fuel warning lights flashing so it came as a great relief when the airstrip appeared. Although it was somewhat shorter than the one we were used to, as it was doubtless very muddy, it would slow us down quickly.

Our arrival caused some concern. A jeep came in a cloud of spray and the driver said that he couldn't promise that we would find our aircraft still intact in the morning: the Japs had been attacking across the airfield every night and the R.A.F. Regiment drove them off each day. As he spoke, the sound of gunfire came from our right and then from our left. I don't know which was the Japs and which was the British but they shelled each other vigorously and we were glad when a 3-tonner arrived and took us to the village.

Then an odd thing happened. We were dropped off in front of a large, single-storey building and I went up to the door and found an Indian servant on duty. I told him we wanted accommodation for the night and he duly conveyed my message to someone inside. A fine-looking man came out, a Group Captain. He was dressed in immaculate khaki drill which was unusual as jungle green was the normal wear in Burma. I said, 'Good evening, sir. We are 34 Squadron. We couldn't get through to our base. Is there somewhere we could stay overnight?'

The Group Captain looked me up and down very slowly. 'Have you got a change of clothes with you? I can't have you in my mess looking like that.'

In the presence of this immaculately dressed officer, I became quite conscious of my own appearance: my jungle green battledress was darkened with sweat; my emergency pair of socks was threaded through my epaulettes; a Smith and Wesson revolver was strapped to the front of my right thigh ; a quart water bottle was dangling from my belt along with a first aid pack ; I had a pouch containing silver Rupees, a holster that I had strapped to my leg, a map, a wallet and various other items right down to my short puttees ending in a pair of large brown boots, with the secret escaper's compass built into one heel and a suicide pill in the other (the suicide pill I planned to drop into a Jap's drinking water).

'I am sorry Sir. We had no room for spare clothing,' I said. 'How many of you are there?'

'Six, sir. Sorry, we lost one. Five actually, sir.'

Behind him a door opened, and I saw several people with drinks in their hands staring at me. I suddenly developed a raging thirst.

'Six Officers,' he said, 'all looking like you?'

I foresaw complications. 'No, five of us, sir, three officers and two N.C.O.s, all 34 Squadron pilots.'

'Oh, well. I will send someone to take you to sick quarters. You can stay there overnight and put your N.C.O.s in the armoury.'

I could hardly believe this was happening. We were being treated like lepers. I thanked him for the accommodation arrangements and then I asked, 'Could we fill our water bottles first, sir?'

The Group Captain looked at me, amazed. He stared at me and said, 'Water? Good God !' Then he turned and walked away. Unfortunately, we were to meet this man again.

That night was very noisy with quite a lot of gunfire and the occasional hand-grenade. I believe this was from the raids by Japanese soldiers who were trying to get to our rations.

The next morning, the sun was shining and we lost no time in getting to the airstrip. Our aircraft stood there, quite unharmed. A bowser came to refuel us which was a slow business as petrol had to be pumped in manually. We looked at the runway. Our flight commander said he had tried to take-off earlier. Steam was rising from the runway and it squelched underfoot.

'Must be bloody mad,' muttered one of the flight sergeants.

Peterson went roaring away and we saw him barely get off the ground at the far end of the airstrip – but it was too late. He ploughed into the trees and chopped the tops of them like cabbages. Someone said, 'Give it another hour. The sun should help.' Nobody thought of going to look for the flight commander: Peterson was not a popular man. About 30 minutes later, a decidely odd-looking figure crept slowly along the airstrip, glistening black from head to foot. It was the flight commander. His T'Bolt had broken up on impact and the oil tank had burst and poured all over him.

I said to him, 'You should go and call on the bastard Group Captain now!'

A couple of hours later we got airborne. The squadron Harvard was sent back to pick up Peterson. This was used mainly to make trips to Calcutta to bring back various items but most importantly, a supply of Lee and Perrins Sauce. The powdered potato we had was quite inedible with a good splash of Lee and Perrins.

Another RAF Thunderbolt, in this case a 30 Squadron Thunderbolt II, taking off from Chittagong in 1944. This aircraft was originally given the US serial number 42-26911, but was, in time, allocated the RAF serial number HD 298. It was written off after becoming involved in a collision with HD 294 on the ground at Chittagong on 17 November 1944. (*San Diego Air and Space Museum*)

Mealtimes provided the occasion for essential heath safeguards. We took our anti-malarial, ephedrine tablets (which dyed our skin a yellowish colour), various vitamin pills and always a large spoonful of salt, washed down immediately with several gulps of water. Salt was essential. We used to make a barrier of Vaseline across our foreheads to prevent the sweat running into our eyes and blinding us. We sweated profusely as we flew and it formed a pool in the seat of our pants. I suppose the Thunderbolt was designed for high altitude work and hadn't called for much in the way of ventilation. There was a pipe between the rudder pedals and a butterfly-valve you worked with your foot. You could direct the soothing jet of air onto your stomach, but that was all.

Some people suffered badly from prickly heat. If this was serious or became infected they had to be grounded . All of us had regular upset

Angus examines the wreckage of a Nakajima Ki-43 Hayabusa, known to the Allies as the Oscar. (*John Gadd Collection*)

stomachs which meant disturbed nights with two or three visits to the latrines, though there wasn't much sleep to disturb as our thick, service mosquito nets made it horribly hot in bed. Occasionally, when you did manage to get to sleep, you would be woken by a nightmare: you were trying to bale out of a plummeting airplane. Your bed would be tipped over, you would be entangled your mosquito net and you woke up in a hell of a state. One American pilot had one of these baling-out dreams and leapt out of a top floor window in the Grand Hotel in Calcutta.

We had plenty of entertainment on the squadron. We played a lot of volleyball and we often played while we waited for take-off. For a bit of adventure, we would wander around the surrounding area to see what we could find. Occasionally, we came across a Japanese soldier who had done a hari-kari job by sticking the muzzle of his rifle under his chin and pulling the trigger with his toe. They were usually in a terrible state of disarray as the vultures had had a go at them.

Chapter 4

Operation *Birdcage*

Now that the Japanese were being pushed back everywhere, it was time for a change in the nature of our employment. Operation *Birdcage* was imminent. This was to be the liberation of Malaya. The role that we were to play was to take over from the Mosquito squadrons patrolling the Burma-Siam railway and to ensure that stayed out of Japanese hands.

We were to move to a place called *Meiktila* in central Burma to the north of Rangoon. News of this came at the end of a day when we were sitting crossed-legged in our little canvas baths, stretched in a line outside our tents. the first in this line was our C.O. This was an exquisitely satisfying experience. We had each been given six half-pint bottles of beer and we sat there, sluicing water over our heads from enamel mugs, taking swigs of beer and chatting happily.

'You'll be seeing an old friend of yours soon, Fin,' the C.O. called out.
'Who's that, sir?'
'Your host of a few weeks ago when you landed at Taungoo.' 'Oh no, sir. Not that bastard!'

The C.O. laughed, 'I'm afraid so. We'll be moving next week and he's the new boss.'

A road convoy took most of our stuff and, on the day of our move, our tents and personal baggage were loaded onto transport aircraft and flown out. We were briefed for a target in the Sittang Bend and after completing this attack we'd fly to base. The weather was fine early in the day but we had no idea when we would be taking off. The sun shone and as we hung around by our aircraft, we exchanged cigarettes for duck eggs with an old Burmese man. We cracked these eggs on the wings of the T'bolts of a neighbouring squadron and they fried in the sun. We wouldn't have done this on our own aircraft as it made quite a bit of a mess. We sliced a loaf of bread and made egg sandwiches.

Thunderbolts taking-off for a sortie in Burma. (*John Gadd Collection*)

Late in the afternoon, we arrived at *Meiktila*. The weather had become very stormy and it took a while to find it. We had a cloud base of about 300 feet and flying a circuit at that height tended to lead to errors in the final approach. One of our chaps, Piggy Ellis, overshot his turn in and tried to correct this in the remaining few seconds. He landed before he had straightened out and his T-Bolt went slithering sideways at more than 100 m.p.h. It hit the monsoon ditch with a tremendous splash and flipped over on its back. The rest of us got down alright and we were glad to find that Piggy wasn't hurt. He was having a cup of tea with us ten minutes later.

Our new Station Commander hadn't taken long to give us a sample of his old nature. He drove up to the crashed aircraft in his jeep, jumped out and levelled his rifle at the cockpit. The idea was that if it went up in flames, he would shoot the pilot. Piggy Ellis told us he could see all this as he hung upside down in the straps and he had his revolver out. In the event of fire he was going to give the Group Captain one first.

A 261 Squadron Thunderbolt II, KL291 coded FJ-S, photographed whilst airborne from Tanjore on May 1945. (*Courtesy of Andrew Thomas*)

Meiktila was a frightful looking dump. The place we had just left had been in the dry zone around Mandalay where we often saw the sun. Here the monsoon prevailed and everything was soggy and saturated or glistening with moisture. We found our tents lying in the mud and got them up before dark. We didn't have time to dig monsoon ditches round them and it rained heavily during the night. The next morning we had to splash around rescuing things from being washed away. Once our mess tent was firmly fixed in place, we sifted through our stack of gramophone records, warped and mouldy as they were, to see which ones had survived the move and soon we had the Andrews Sisters singing *Sho sho baby* followed by several other favourites.

That afternoon, we were sitting in the mess when the Group Captain appeared. He had his rifle under his arm. He had been told that Jap raids were very prevalent in this area and so he always carried his rifle. It wasn't the usual service Enfield rifle but a rather posh sort of sporting rifle.

He strolled towards us and, as I happened to be the nearest, I stood and said, 'Good afternoon, sir.'

'What are you?' he said with a great sneer. 'I'm a 34 Squadron pilot, sir,' I said.

'I know that,' he replied, 'but what are you? Are you Flying Officer, an Air Commodore, or what?'

The point was now clear. It was necessary to avoid prickly heat so we only ever wore a towel and sandals during the day. We were doing our best to keep fit for flying.

A voice behind me said, 'I'm the Squadron Commander, sir. Shall we talk outside?' Gavin Douglas our C.O. went out and had a furious row with the Group Captain. Douglas was a splendid man he had been a cavalry officer in the Indian Army before the war. He came back and said to us, 'I'm grounding the whole squadron. None of you are to fly.' Then he stormed off to his tent, got dressed and drove off to Rangoon in his jeep.

The Station Commander continued to interfere. He said we were to take-off and land west to east, but there was a better approach from the east and we wanted to keep it that way. He tried to interfere with our Sergeant's Mess arrangements and we wouldn't stand for that either. One night in the mess, a few old hands were quietly discussing the situation. Morale had been getting shaky and that was the sort of thing that would cause accidents.

'We have got to get rid of him,' someone said. 'Well, how the hell?' asked another.

'I'll show you. Wait a minute.'

The man went off to his tent and came back a few minutes later with a Japanese rifle. He put a single round in it, pointed it at the ground and bang, off it went. There was a neat little hole in the floor of the tent.

'That's how,' he said.

I felt a bit nervous at this. There was clearly something wrong with shooting someone other than a clearly defined enemy. I said so but my protest was dismissed.

'That man is an enemy. He's a killer and he doesn't mind who he kills.' Someone got some straws and broke them into small pieces. The newer members of the squadron, myself included, were not offered the chance to participate. Just three or four of these hard-drinking, jungly old hands took part in the draw.

A Thunderbolt I of 113 Squadron, that coded AD-R, pictured at Ondaw in April 1945. (*Courtesy of Andrew Thomas*)

A few days later, our much-hated Station Commander challenged us to a volleyball game. His team of headquarters staff made a very poor show against us and we absolutely thrashed them. The Group Captain was furious and swore at his team every time when they missed a pass. Then he accused us of unfair tactics so we offered a re-play. He just stormed off in a foul temper.

That night, a strong force of tribesmen raided the camp and there was a lot of gunfire. Someone mentioned the next day that the Group Captain had stood at the door of his caravan – a nice, dry, comfortable caravan – holding his rifle at the ready and with a light shining behind him.

'So,' they said, 'makes you think doesn't it? You only have to do that once too often …'

These attacks were not particularly dangerous affairs because the gunfire and the noise it made was simply to divert attention from the raiding parties who were sneaking in, trying to steal parachutes and anything else that might be of use to them. Understandably, their womenfolk liked the parachute silk for making clothing.

Operation Birdcage *71*

A Thunderbolt II of 30 Squadron photographed at Jumchar on 15 January 1945. (*Courtesy of Andrew Thomas*)

I don't remember exactly when the war came to an end. The dropping of the atom bombs and the Japanese surrender were a ragged affair. The Japs in Burma were not observing the ceasefire so attacks on them had to continue. Even on the day the surrender documents were signed, they executed a large number of people in Singapore. The small parties of Japanese who had been heading for the escape route through the Sittang Bend, where over 12,000 of their soldiers had been killed, brought a new terror to Burmese civilians. With a kind of vindictive savagery, they killed the Burmese as they went along in variety of unpleasant ways, women and children – anyone they could get hold of.

Our C.O. who had now managed to curtail the Station Commander's interference, called us together to emphasise the great care needed as the monsoon had its final fling. Aircraft losses had risen considerably over the previous month. Twelve supply-dropping Dakotas had been lost due to the weather and, over the battlefield, vultures were an increasing nuisance attracted by the thousands of dead Japs. Hitting one of those could easily cause a fatal accident.

The fate of one RAF Thunderbolt in Burma – in this case another 113 Squadron aircraft, coded AD-D. From December 1944 until the end of the war, Nos. 34 and 113 squadrons shared a number of facilities and frequently operated from the same airfield. (*Courtesy of Andrew Thomas*)

Thunderbolt Squadrons were having suffering some mysterious losses at this time. Obviously, we weren't now losing any from the high-speed dive situation: there simply wasn't enough clear sky to make a high-speed dive, and we had, by this time, received an explanation for that. There was a document, headed 'Compressibility' which showed that a Thunderbolt could lock – up in a dive and produce odd effects such as control reversal. The simple solution to that was to avoid high speeds at high altitudes. Later versions of the aircraft were fitted with air brakes which resolved the issue. I wonder how many of the thirteen test pilots who were killed in the development of the Thunderbolt came unstuck due to that particular snag.

The new problem, however, was quite baffling. The aircraft just exploded . A clue to this mystery had already been noticed but it had been ignored. I experienced it myself one day. I was flying along quite normally when there was a loud bang and the aircraft shook violently.

One of the leaflets that were dropped as part of Operation Birdcage to inform the Burmese population that the War against Japan had ended. (*John Gadd Collection*)

The throttle lever was blown back several inches. My No. 2 called up and said he had just seen a big puff of smoke come from my supercharger housing but we didn't give this a second thought.

The cease-fire was eventually enforced in the immediate battle zone but now we had to drop leaflets in isolated areas telling the Japs and Burmese that the war was over. This involved some very long flights and external fuel tanks were fitted giving us a seven-hour duration.

The fact was that this was far too long. Even after three hours our quart water bottles were empty and we were always very thirsty. We had pilots losing consciousness and crashing. I thought of their families, relieved that the war was over and expecting them home.

We also had to try and reach places in mountainous territory. Just two of us would go on these trips but we would find ourselves in cloud and mountains, and they don't mix well. We would split up and climb as steeply as we could at full power. Hard-looking bits of mountain flashed passed, inches from our wing tips, and the sweat seemed to squirt out of your armpits as you sat there expecting an enormous impact at any moment. Eventually, you would break cloud and, in the distance, see the other chap casting around for a bit of clear sky below but there wasn't any. Now the problem was how to get back to base. A descent over land would be well-nigh suicidal so you'd slog off south until you thought you were well out over the Gulf then creep down feeling for the sea. Cloud and sea were the same colour so you had to be very careful. Once there, it was a simple matter to pick up the coastline and work your way back.

One day, I set out on one of these long-range trips but we didn't get very far before the chap I was with had a fuel-pressure problem and we had to turn back. I had been offered a lift to Rangoon the next day in a jeep and I had been looking forward to this. Now it seemed that we would have undertake this long-range trip again.

The Flight Commander, looked at me very meanly and said, 'You've been doing too much flying lately. Someone else can take your aircraft. You can stay on the ground.' I smiled to myself. I could see he thought this would upset me, but dropping leaflets was a bit of a bore.

Shortly after I arrived back from Rangoon I was told, 'You've lost your T'Bolt, Fin. It blew up.'

Two aircraft had flown along the Malay Peninsular in clear weather, dropped their leaflets and turned to fly back. Just at that moment, my

Angus photographed this wreckage of an Allied Beaufighter during his time in Burma. Unfortunately, the identity of both the aircraft and the location has not been recorded. (*John Gadd Collection*)

Inspecting the remains of what appears to be a 5 Squadron Curtiss Mohawk in the summer of 1945. (*John Gadd Collection*)

T'Bolt, flown by the flight sergeant, turned to head north when it exploded in a great ball of orange flame and black smoke. I felt more remorse than relief. It should have been me and I'd been swanning around in Rangoon.

Soon after this, the mystery was solved. Knowing how vital it was to have tanks filled to the brim, no thought had been given to the expansion of this fuel in the heat. The tanks were therefore splitting, and several gallons of fuel were sloshing around ready to be ignited right beneath the aeroplane. It only needed the fuel to touch a very hot part of the aircraft and up it went.

One other thing became clear too. The old Indian fortune-teller had said someone called Peters would do me a favour. Peters/ Peterson. It was pretty close, but favours that cost somebody else's life aren't worth having. I came across that old Indian fortune-teller when I was in Calcutta on business a few years after the war. He recognised me and said simply, 'You've come back.' He didn't want to linger over this meeting but as he moved away, he turned and said, 'In your new job, be careful of one JA.' He was right there as well.

There was quite a brisk tribal raid one night and, under cover of all the noise, it was obvious that the man who had drawn the short straw was awaiting his chance. At breakfast the following morning, people were whispering and laughing and glancing at each other in an odd way. I found out what it was about later. I took an opportunity to walk past the Group Captain's caravan and take a close look. About 4 feet up in the door frame was a bullet hole. It had missed its target by about 10 inches. I was to have another encounter with this Station Commander soon after which brought an end to my days on 34 Squadron, although the squadron was already within a few weeks of disbanding.

I had to do a 'committee of adjustment' on one of our flight sergeants who had crashed. It was a job I thoroughly disliked – in fact I hated it. All his possessions had to be checked through and items of sentimental interest returned to his next of kin. This meant reading through his diary and letters and getting rid of anything that might not reflect very well on him. It was a horrible job. Then the remaining odds and ends of personal effects were rounded up and auctioned in the Sergeants' Mess with the proceeds being sent to his next of kin. This auction was the one bright spot in the whole show. It was a magnificent tribute to a fallen comrade.

Operation Birdcage 77

One of 34 Squadron's Thunderbolt IIs, KJ201, which was coded EG-F, at Zayatkwin in September 1945. His logbook reveals that Angus flew this aircraft on a combat sortie on 28 July 1945. (*Courtesy of Andrew Thomas*)

As the auctioneer, I would hold up some insignificant item, say a pencil for example, 'Now what am I bid for this top-quality Venus HB pencil. 20 rupees shall I say? 15 over there. Come along now, come along. It must be worth more than that. It's got Lofty's teeth marks in the end. 20 rupees over there. Thank you, Bill,' and so it would go on. The pencil would eventually sell for, say, 100 rupees or about £7, and the auction went on for hours.

Every minute of it seemed like a tribute to our dead friend. Someone would pass up a nearly full bottle of Scotch.

'Put that in for me,' he would say. When I sold it, it would be immediately put up again, with a proviso that I took a swig which I duly did. 'Not enough,' came the cry, 'have another'.

So, I would have another. In the end I'd finish up buying this thing myself so that I could put the cork in it while I was still able to stand. At one stage I lost my balance and to the delight of the crowd I fell through

The fate of a 34 Squadron Thunderbolt II, KL341 coded EG-U, at Zayatkwin on 7 October 1945. The pilot on this occasion was Geoff Sorrell, who had flown alongside Angus. (*Courtesy of Andrew Thomas*)

the side of the tent and into the monsoon ditch! Dripping wet, I climbed back and carried on. Around midnight, one of the less intoxicated chaps came up and said there was trouble outside the tent. A pilot who had just popped outside for a moment had found the Group Captain there.

I arrived just in time. The Group Captain was livid but he couldn't have chosen a worse time to interfere in things. Chaps surged out of the tent and began yelling abuse at him. He told me to fetch our commanding officer. I was very much the worse for wear but I managed to clear my head. I said, 'I am going to your caravan, sir. I'll see you there,' and I lurched off. He came along and we had a terrific slanging match. He told me I was a disgrace to the service and that I should be ashamed of myself. Well that did it. I let rip.

A line-up of RAF Thunderbolts in Burma. From the placement of a similar image in Angus's logbook, it would appear that these aircraft are from 42 Squadron and were photographed in late 1945. (*John Gadd Collection*)

Groundcrew 'bombing up' RAF Thunderbolts in Burma. Again, from the placement of a similar image in Angus's logbook, it would appear that these aircraft are from 42 Squadron and were photographed in late 1945. (*John Gadd Collection*)

He said that he was going to have me arrested and I told him that he would have a riot on his hands if that happened.

Next morning, things moved fast, I was quickly hustled into the squadron Harvard and posted up to 42 Squadron.

Pretty soon after I got there, I went off on leave to a place up in the hills from Mandalay, rather like a British suburb and the squadron had a house there, 'T'Bolt House'. I spent a very pleasant week there and when I came back to the squadron, I found that too was disbanding and a tremendous party had been planned for all ranks.

I took a T'bolt, from which all the guns had been removed, back to my old airfield where the bar stocks from my old squadron had come up for sale. I handed over a great, fat wad of money, packed the bottles into the wings of the T'bolt and headed back. A colossal party for all ranks followed.

A Thunderbolt II, KL300 coded AD-R, of 113 Squadron at Kwetnge, April 1945. (*Courtesy of Andrew Thomas*)

A 113 Squadron Thunderbolt II, with the serial number KL839 and coded AD-A, in Burma in the middle of 1945. (*Courtesy of Andrew Thomas*)

Thunderbolt II KL849, a 161 Squadron aircraft coded FJ-G, pictured whilst airborne from Myingyan during May 1945. The pilot on this occasion was Squadron Leader R.H. Fletcher. (*Courtesy of Andrew Thomas*)

Chapter 5

Spitfire!

After this I was posted to Bhopal in northern India and, going back via Calcutta, I experienced the strange sensation of walking on hard pavements again after months of walking on bare earth. The contrast was quite remarkable. It was just as marked as seeing the greenness of England after the winter white of Canada.

At Bhopal, there was quite an assortment of aircraft. There were some Thunderbolts present but also Spitfires and Tempests. I got into a Spitfire flight. It was the Mark 9 we had there, a tropical version with more efficient cooling. I was very happy to be flying a Spit at last – a classic finish to my flying experience. It was a most delightful aeroplane, a sheer joy. We performed a wide variety of exercises such as low-level cross-country flights, in which timing and navigation had to be spot-on in order to rendezvous with other low-level aircraft. An error of 10 seconds was the maximum permitted for a successful rendezvous.

We also did some dive-bombing. I had never thought of the Spitfire as a dive-bomber but it was perfectly satisfactory, though not as steady as a T'Bolt and nowhere near as fast in the dive. It had one peculiarity which it was as well to remember. Unless you loaded the elevator trim nose-heavy before you went into your dive, just as you were pulling out, she tightened up and you'd had it. There was no question of making a quick grab at the trim control: your hands were so heavy with G-loading you could hardly move them. Then you blacked out.

I only made this mistake once. When I recovered consciousness, I couldn't think what was happening. The aircraft had zoomed up and I woke to find it upside down, climbing away quite happily in a slight turn. It came under full control again as soon as I took things in hand. Bill Brooks, another Spitfire pilot, had a real tight one. His head jerked down so violently as he blacked out, he hit the gunsight and, despite the rubber padding, he received a cut on his forehead. The strain on the

PILOTS ON CONVERSION COURSE TO SPITFIRE Mk. V111 BHOPAL INDIA OCT/NOV 1945
Ex 113 Sqdn. F/S Boyton-Salts. F/S Carpenter. F/S Gray. F/Lt Slinger. F/O Proud
W/O Bedbrook. F/O PGW. F/O Ellis. F/S Ferguson. Top Row.

Ex 34 Sqdn. W/O Dark. F/O Sorrell. F/O Mason. F/O Dawkins. W/O Hudson.
F/O Bailey. F/S Sheehan. Bottom Row.

A group photograph of pilots from Nos. 34 and 113 squadrons pictured at Bhopal, India, in October 1945 during conversion to the Spitfire. A number of these men are mentioned in 34 Squadron's Operations Record Book and flew alongside Angus. (*Courtesy of Andrew Thomas*)

airframe had been tremendous. I ran a finger along the mainplane and it bumped up and down over the rippled metal skin. I doubt if that aircraft ever flew again.

While we were at Bhopal, the political situation in India was really on the boil. The fear was that it would bubble over. Arrangements for India's independence were well under way but it looked as if the Indians were not going to wait and they might snatch it at any moment. There had also been a lot of trouble with strikes and mutinies on R.A.F. stations owing to the slowness of in repatriation, though I believe there was agitation was behind it and this was being investigated by special police bought out from England.

One way and another, the situation was a bit delicate. In this respect, I made the most appalling error – and one which could have had terrible consequences.

On my first dive-bombing exercise, I pressed the button to call up the range but got no reply. Straight away I transmitted again with the same result. I was just about to try again when something occurred to me and, banking the Spitfire, I looked at the ground I had just flown over. There they were two columns of smoke from the bombs I had just dropped, slap in the middle of an Indian village. The button on the throttle was the bomb release, not – as in the Thunderbolt – the radio transmitter button. Embarrassment was not the word for it. As I flew back to base at full throttle, I thought a student of history would one day be asked, 'How was the great massacre of the British in India started by an R.A.F. pilot in 1946?'

Immediately on landing, I grabbed a phone and got the Station Security Officer. He was worried enough as it was, having to prepare his defence plans for the station. I thought this would just about finish him off. However, he took the news very calmly and within a few minutes we were identifying the village on the map. It was too small to be named but I had fixed its exact position.

He rang the civilian police headquarters and said, 'Two bombs have accidently dropped from one of our aircraft. If you have got a map, I will tell you exactly where they fell. They were just little practice bombs but someone may have noticed smoke so I thought I had better tell you.' He winked at me.

A few minutes later the security officer said, 'No harm done then.' 'I see thank you very much Inspector…., I'm sorry, I didn't get

your name. Inspector Gobdar. Thank you very much. Goodbye.'

He put the phone down and turned to me and said, 'That was damn lucky. The whole village was evacuated last week; outbreak of plague. Orders have been given for it to be burnt.'

Mutiny cropped up in an unexpected quarter a week later. I was playing tennis one afternoon when a continuous stream of aircraft took off and departed. We never flew in the afternoon so this was a very odd thing to happen but we didn't let it interfere with our game. A couple of hours later we had had a bath and we were sitting outside our hut, drinking tea, when a jeep came roaring up and the Station Adjutant shouted, 'The Indian Navy's mutinied! They're going to blow up Bombay. Get in.'

At Station Headquarters, the Commanding Officer, a Group Captain Fields, said he wanted me to organise all of our Harvards to carry ammunition to Bombay. The aircraft had left in too much of a hurry to arm their guns. There was only one problem: a Harvard couldn't carry enough fuel to get to Bombay. However, provided we had no head wind, we might just get to Poona, re-fuel there and thereby reach Bombay.

Our ground crews responded splendidly. All their mutinous feelings subsided and they worked all night to get the aircraft ready. There was no lighting in the hangars so we had rows of 3-ton trucks lined up outside shining their headlights inside. At dawn we had three Harvards crammed with ammunition and off we went.

A Harvard's duration is three hours and the first part of the flight took exactly that. Our engines cut out just as we landed at Poona. The airfield was crowded with hastily assembled aircraft and, as a hint to the Indian sailors, a varied assortment of aircraft flew over the harbour. To this day, I'm not sure what the mutiny was about. It was understood that the ships had their guns trained on the Taj Mahal Hotel. One of our officers happened to be there for his honeymoon . He had married an army nurse at Bhopal.

I received a message from our Group Captain saying, 'Bring out Flying Officer Shanks and wife from Taj Mahal.' I was told that Army vehicles were being stoned by wild mobs in the streets so I had no chance of making the journey. It was a non-starter.

A couple of days later, the whole thing had calmed down and I flew back to Bhopal. Things were generally much quieter though they were livened up briefly by an interesting Thunderbolt crash. This was a case of engine failure on final approach. He hadn't enough height to reach the runway and, just short of the runway, there was a large hollow with a number of single-storey brick buildings. His descent would have carried him into these buildings. Just in front of the buildings was a patch of rough ground. He rapidly shoved the nose even further down and aimed for this. He must have hit the ground at about 160 m.p.h. Bits of Thunderbolt sailed into the air and fell back to earth. When we arrived on the scene three to four minutes later, there was only one recognisable object. The fuselage had snapped off immediately behind and in front of the cockpit and the wings had also broken off. But there, dusting himself down, next to this perfectly intact but amputated cockpit, was the pilot with nothing but a tiny scratch on his face: a good example of how well a T'bolt would look after you in a crash.

More Spitfire experience lay ahead. I received orders to join 28 Squadron at Kuala Lumpur as Adjutant and there I was to find Gavin Douglas, my 34 Squadron C.O., in command.

The journey from India to Malaya included a pleasant voyage aboard a small ship, the *Navasa*. We sailed first to Singapore and from there to Kuala Lumpur.

No. 28 was one of the long-established, Far East Squadrons. In the 1930 s, it had served on the North-West Frontier. In Burma, it was a tactical reconnaissance squadron using Hurricanes . We had been stationed together at one of my old airfields and I remember one of their very wild parties before we left for Burma.

In Kuala Lumpur, we had the Griffin engined Spit 14s and here I must come down on the side of those who say that, through their greatly increased power, these later Marks lost a lot of charm. The horsepower was just about doubled. It was still a magnificent aircraft but the magic had gone. The flow of power to the five-blade airscrews was collosal and the rudder pedal had to be pushed until it was at full stretch for take-off. At this point, if you wanted to frighten people and risk an interview with the station commander, you could go straight into a series of climbing rolls.

In normal flight, the power setting was kept steady with no need for frequent variation. However, handling a Spit 14 in a large formation in bumpy air was very tiresome. The constant changes in the pressure of the spiral of air around the fuselage meant that the rudder was kicking back at you all the time. One oddity which caused a lot of amusement for spectators was that the engine had a very fast tick-over and, to slow down after landing, it was sometimes necessary to operate the cut-out and let the engine almost stop. This was only necessary in a stream landing when half a dozen or so Spitfires were coming in and there was no taxi track at the end of the runway to turn on to.

Findon at the controls of a Spitfire Mk.XIV whilst flying over the Burmese jungle. He first flew this type, whilst with 28 Squadron, on 14 May 1946. (*John Gadd Collection*)

It was like landing on an aircraft carrier in this respect: the aircraft congregated at the far end and then all taxied back along the runway after the last one had landed.

Inevitably, someone wouldn't switch the cut-out off in time to get the engine to pick up and, on this fairly narrow airstrip, there wasn't much space for the remaining aircraft to squeeze past, if one or more of the Spitfires had come to a standstill. This produced some tense moments and much excitement for the spectators.

In a sudden surge of demobilisation, all but a few of the 28 Squadron pilots were on the boat, heading for home. We mustered a few Spitfires to seek out their troop ship in the Malacca Straits and beat it up in a farewell salute.

The new C.O., Peter Wycombe, didn't seem at all pleased with his lot and he would often glance at me across the office and ask, 'Where can we get a drink, Fin?'

'At half past nine in the morning, sir?'

A Spitfire Mk.XIV of 28 Squadron being warmed up prior to take-off, July 1946. (*John Gadd Collection*)

Pete was a remarkable man and I think he probably had more single-engine, operational flying time than any pilot in any air force – over 700 hours. He flew Gloucester Gladiators; I think that was in Greece and, towards the end of the war in Europe, he led an American Mustang Wing which was largely concerned with strikes against enemy shipping in the North Sea and along the Scandinavian Coast. His decorations included the Distinguished Service Order, Distinguished Flying Cross and Bar and the American Silver Star which must be quite a rare distinction for an R.A.F. officer.

He told me an amazing story. One day he found himself flying over France with no other aircraft in sight and he had no idea what he was supposed to be doing. He looked around for a few minutes and then turned round and flew back to his base in England and landed.

He was told he had to go to the bar and decided to fetch a friend to join the party but, instead of getting into his jeep, he had walked straight past it, climbed into his Mustang, took off and flew away. He had reached the stage were there was virtually no difference between getting into an aeroplane or getting into a jeep.

On becoming C.O. of 28 Squadron, Pete Wycombe had had to accept a reduction in rank from Wing Commander to Squadron Leader. He should have been in a much higher job but he never went out of his way to be popular with the Air Ministry and he had no respect for rank.

I was happy to discover, years later, that he became A.O.C. Far East and worked closely with General Templar in the jungle warfare which was such a great threat to the stability of Malaya.

Chapter 6

Last Days

Looking back on my time in Malaya, if I had those days again, I'd do better to sign the pledge before I started. Drink featured too largely in our lives and each night, until well past midnight, there was a ghastly, hard-drinking party.

There was one unfortunate incident in my time with 28 Squadron. A pilot, posted from Hong Kong, came just in time to solve a problem. We had a Spit 14 on the squadron which was needed in India but we had nobody with enough hours on type to undertake a ferry trip

-until this Hong Kong pilot arrived. The poor chap found himself on the move straight away. A Mosquito was detailed to escort him there via Bangkok. Why the escort ended in Southern Burma I don't know, but as soon as he reached Burma, he was on his own and that was the last we ever heard of him. The monsoon had chalked up another victim.

It had never occurred to me that I might fly in a peace-time air force. Peace was something that appeared to be getting scarce again in the early 1950 s. The Korean War began while I was working in India and I responded to an appeal for volunteers to form a group to go there as an Indian contribution. I had hoped the Americans would let us have some Mustangs but that never got beyond the United Nations Delhi Office.

My health at the time was rapidly getting worse so I had to leave India anyway as I had been told I wouldn't live through another hot season in Calcutta. Back in England, with the help of the Hospital for Tropical Disease, I recovered and re-joined the R.A.F.

The type of commissions available then were branch list, with a promotion barrier of flight lieutenant rank, or short service commission for eight years. There was no chance at all of a permanent commission. I wasn't going to accept the limitation of the branch list proposition so I took the eight-year contract, which would doubtless have been enough for any active work that might crop up.

CENTRAL FLYING SCHOOL

This is to Certify that

FG. OFF. A. FINDON.

has successfully graduated from the Central Flying School as a Qualified Flying Instructor

DATE 10-9-52

COMMANDANT

The certificate presented to Angus on his graduation from the Central Flying School, as a qualified flying instructor, on 10 September 1952. (*John Gadd Collection*)

I was slightly disappointed at finding myself on a flying instructor's course at Little Rissington and not at all pleased at being sent to the R.A.F. College at Cranwell, mainly because I wanted to be amid better countryside than Lincolnshire. So far as the work was concerned, naturally I did this to the best of my ability. Somewhere a potential enemy pilot was being trained and I wanted to be sure that my pupil would be the better of the two. Also, one had to produce a safe pilot for the benefit of the people who might be his crew or passengers and no effort was spared to achieve this.

I made a bit of a nuisance of myself in an effort to get away from Lincolnshire. I took a Chipmunk over to a Butlins Holiday Camp on the coast and gave it a thorough beating up, then I flew round a few times to make sure they got my number – but I wasn't reported.

I came closer to official displeasure up at Driffield where I joined a cheerful crowd of ex-wartime, ex-sergeant pilots for a fortnight flying Meteors. I had already flown a Vampire at Little Rissington – my first experience of jet aircraft – and I didn't find Meteors any less boring. I disliked their smell and the hideous noise they inflicted on people and I didn't like being monitored from base all the time. A voice would suddenly tell you, 'Driffield Charlie Victor, you have been airborne 20 minutes.' This contrasted so greatly with the independence and responsibility I had always enjoyed as a single-engine pilot.

I took off on an exercise one day but I sensed something was not quite right so I didn't go up through the cloud. I flew along at about 2,000 feet trying to puzzle it out. Then I found it. It was nothing serious but, in a routine glance at my instruments, I became fascinated by the movement of the fuel-gauge needles. To see your fuel level actually falling before your eyes was something new and made me feel quite uncomfortable. I hadn't realised that, at low level, a jet engine consumes such enormous quantities so very quickly. I soon abandoned the idea of the exercise I was supposed to be doing and just stooged around.

Visibility was not too great so I decided to test one of the navigational aids available on the radio. I chose the position-finding one and was most impressed with the result. In no time at all I was told I was 35 miles South West of Spurn Head, but it then occurred to me that this didn't help a great deal unless you had a pretty good idea where Spurn Head was.

Gloster Meteor T.Mk.7 WG962 photographed by Angus during his time at the Central Flying School. This aircraft crashed on 26 June 1962, when the engine failed during take-off from RAF Little Rissington, Gloucestershire. It rolled into ground, killing both members of the crew. (*John Gadd Collection*)

I checked my chart and worked out a course for base, watching the ground ahead of me to check my position. This is not the way to fly a jet. Spending most of the time above cloud, a jet pilot uses the radio and depends on it at all times. I thought it was time to get an accurate steer for home and Driffield came back to me with a course which confirmed my present heading. However, I still hadn't identified a landmark and I needed this to make a calculation on distance for remaining fuel.

Driffield was thinking the same. They came back and asked me my fuel state. As I was passing them the rather gloomy details, I suddenly saw a murky bit of water and a smudge of built-up area in front of me. It was the Humber near Grimsby.

Driffield now called again and asked me if I knew my position. What I didn't know was that the sweat was starting to flow down there in the control room. Meteor losses had reached an alarming rate. There was no clear reason for this but the press was making a meal of it which was having a detrimental effect on recruitment and the Air Ministry were very unhappy.

At Driffield, they were in a bit of a twitch and the Station Commander was already in the control-room seeing his prospects of promotion going down the drain. I told them that I was just crossing the Humber. They then asked me what I thought was a remarkably stupid question. They said, 'Do you know how far you are from base?'

I wasn't going to stick my head back in the office to look at the map at this stage. I said to them, 'Yes, I do – about as far as you are from the Humber.' This remark, coming over the control room loudspeaker, produced a situation I would have liked to have seen. Apparently, the Station Commander shook with rage and those around him quaked and turned pale.

On landing and giving them back their Meteor all in one piece, I was immediately summoned to the office of Wing Commander Flying, who was still trembling and kept repeating, 'The Group Captain was livid, absolutely livid.' I was then grounded for the remainder of my stay at Driffield. Something a lot worse would probably have happened but coming from Cranwell worked to my advantage. A Cranwell Staff Officer was a bit of a sacred cow in the Royal Air Force.

Much of my off-duty time at Cranwell was devoted to the Beagle Pack for which I was hunt secretary, treasurer, and whipper-in. The Master – Group Captain, later Air Commodore, Levis – was, at the time, president of the selection-board and he good-naturedly put up with my complaints about the quality of cadets for pilot training.

After Cranwell, I was posted to Syerston where we flew piston-engine Provosts. The Jet Provost was as uninspiring as the Vampire and Meteor and, at Syerston we trained Fleet Air Arm pilots. This was a very happy station until there was a change of command. It fell to me as Mess Secretary to spearhead the reaction to this unpopular new Station Commander and when it reached the point of fairly militant attacks on each other, I was posted.

I became the Flying Adjutant at the Central Flying School, Little Rissington. We had quite a bit if fun there with the R.A.F. aerobatic team, then known as the Pelicans – the Pelican being the main feature of the Central Flying School crest. When we changed from Meteors to Hunters, the name also changed: we became the Red Arrows. There were some doubts about this name at the time due to the obvious political interpretations of anything red.

Finally, I was given command of the Communications Flight at the Central Flying School. I ended my days with the R.A.F. very happily. I'll share one last memory of that place.

The Flight Sergeant in charge of servicing was always very stressed. It used to bother me that he got in such a tizz about things and always looked so worried. I set about trying to make him unflappable.

One day, he came to my office, saluted and looked at me very hard and said with great calmness, 'The Anson's just gone up, sir.'

'Oh, good. Where's she gone?' I said.

'Nowhere, sir. She's just gone up in flames.'

I caught sight of the smug look of satisfaction in his eyes as he watched me leap out of my chair and rush out of the office at full speed.

Appendix I

Extract From No.34 Squadron Operations Record Book – Summary of Events, June to September 1945

June 1945

Kinmagan (Burma)

Operations.   Once again operations have been severely restricted by the weather. On moving to Kinmagan in the early days of the month, we thought it would be possible to carry out at least one mission a day, but after six aircraft had successfully attacked Japanese positions at Bhamo, on the Mawchi Road, on the 5th, operations were completely suspended until the 22nd, owing to the unserviceability of the strip through heavy rains. Even when the strip became serviceable the remaining five operations of the month were abortive due to adverse weather mainly in the Toungoo area. A most disappointing month as the following figures show:

Operational Sorties	36
Operational Flying Hours	76 hrs 30 mins
No. of bombs dropped	12 × 500lbs
No. of rounds of ammo expended	7260 × 5

Administration.   On the first of the month, on the instructions of H.Q. 221 Group, the Squadron moved by road from Kwetnge, there to come under the administration of H.Q. Wing. The shortage of pilots on the Unit has been eased by the posting in of the following, all Thunderbolt O.T.U. trained pilots:

F/O Tedder
P/O Findon
F/Sgt Dark
F/Sgt Holloway
Sgt Littlewood
Sgt Thwaits
Sgt Soper
Sgt Sheehan
Sgt Hornsey

Appendix I 97

Medical.	The Officer in Medical Charge reports "During the month 12 pilots reported sick. There was no preponderance of any one disease and only 9 days flying were lost as a result. The sharp outbreak of diarrhoea at Kwetnge subsided on the move to Kinmagan. Deep trench latrines are in use and are sprayed weekly with D.D.T. Very few flies are to be found around the latrines or on the camp generally."
Daily Diary.	
Kwetnge	
1st	The move to Kinmagan is now under way. The pilots proceeded by road, the aircraft having been flown to the new strip last month (It will be remembered that because of the heavy rains at Kwetnge the kites were flown out at the earliest opportunity to Myingyan and a little later were transferred to Kinmagan, the pilots returning to Kwetnge).
2nd	The move is being carried out by road with a limited number of vehicles, consequently it will take several days to transport the whole of our servicing echelon. Parties of 30 odd men are sent off every day. Of the Squadron, the C.O., Adjutant and the Intelligence Officer are remaining behind to see that everything goes off according to plan.
3rd	F/Lt Paddle, who has been held up through transport difficulties, returned from Ranchi where he has been discussing training problems. F/O R.W. Williams also returned from the same place unsuccessfully completing a V.C.P. Course.
4th	The C.O. left for the new strip. F/O J.M.N. Verschoyle-Campbell (Pilot) arrived from 28 Squadron on posting.
Kinmagan	From the new strip, the Squadron carried out its first operation of the month. Six pilots took part, four of them being "Old Timers" who had been doing close support work for the army all the way from Tamu to Rangoon. Today's job was very attractive and was welcomed by all. 300 of the enemy were reported to be clustered in the village of Bhamo and our job was to wipe them out and to attack any likely positions to the East. It was midday when the twelve bombs were released over the village. Two exploded bang in the centre, two on the West side and two overshoots slightly to the West. Four found targets on the S.E. side. One hang up fell on the village during the subsequent strafing runs. Dust made it impossible to observe the results of the bombing, but many strikes were seen during the strafing and two bashas were left smouldering. The

	pilots were very enthusiastic on their return and considered it a most successful attack.
5th	The Adjutant and the Intelligence Officer left for Kinmagan, thus completing the move.
6th	Flying is temporarily at an end because of the unserviceability of the strip.
7th	Nine Thunderbolt trained pilots arrived on posting from 8 R.F.U. Although they have done no previous operations, they are very good material and provided the strip will permit some practice flying they should soon be fit for operations.
8th	Ten of our pilots who have not been converted to P.47's (and have little opportunity of converting on the Unit) left for H.Q. R.A.F. Burma for disposal.
9th	Very heavy rains flooded the whole camp.
10th	In spite of the frequent rains, the weather is very hot and this, combined with the peculiar laxative qualities tends to reduce one's inclination to work. The C.O. however has by his own example induced the other pilots to put in some hard work on the Ante Room, which is now looking quite homely.
11th	Since December 1944, 34 and 113 Squadrons have shared a joint officers' mess. The many moves made by both squadrons since that date have seriously depleted the mess crockery cupboard, and so at a mess meeting held this evening it was decided to send F/O Leng to Calcutta to buy replacements.
12th	W/O Popplewell, a pilot who has been with the Squadron some 18 months and has participated in many attacks on the enemy during that period, proceeded to Rangoon to represent the Squadron on the Victory Parade. With him went F/O R.W. Williams to be interviewed by the S.A.S.O. 221 Group regarding his V.C.P. Course.
13th	The Adjutant left for Calcutta by air; P/O Soulsby took over his duties.
14th	Posting through for P/O L. Soulsby. He is to go on an Airborne V.C.P. Course. F / O Tedder will now occupy the Adjutant's chair.
15th	On the domestic side we are now well settled at Kinmagan. It is a well organised station and boasts a first-class cinema. Operationally the strip is a dead loss as it is not fit for practice flying even.
16th	F/Lt M. Hodsman who doesn't take Mepacrines went sick with Malaria.
17th	W/O Reid and W/O Colwill took off in the Harvard for Calcutta. Arriving at Cox's Baxaar, the undercarriage failed

Appendix I 99

	and a prang resulted. The two pilots escaped without injury and continued the journey by D.C. P/O L. Soulsby left for Ranchi on attachment, and managed to get a lift as far as Calcutta in a Mosquito. Three left on attachment to 79 Squadron who are very short of pilots at the moment.
19th	The strip is now serviceable for practice flying (no bombs being carried) and today a number of the new pilots were given a try-out.
20th/21st	Intensive training for the new people; they are shaping well. On the 21st F/O Williams returned from Rangoon, bringing with him some of our overdue beer ration.
22nd	The strip has improved slightly and consequently, in the morning six pilots briefed to strafe 600 of the enemy known to be gathered at points PT 2789 and QB 343896 and also a betelnut plantation on the East slope of these areas. The aircraft reached Thaveba (QB 0991) but the weather here was so bad they had to call it a day and return to base, the mission unaccomplished.
23rd	Operations were again attempted today, but again the weather rendered the mission abortive. This time 6 aircraft set out to strafe likely areas 30 miles East of Toungoo on the Toungoo-Mawchi Road. The target area was reached but the actual targets could not be located because of the prevailing weather conditions. No more training flights were carried out.
24th/25th	These two days were spent on further training. The C.O. made his first solo on Thunderbolts.
26th	Another abortive sortie. Six aircraft detailed to attack an enemy camp 25 miles East of Toungoo got as far as Pyinmana and had to turn back because of weather.
27th	Six aircraft again set out to attack yesterday's targets but, encountered bad weather near Yezin.
28th	Reports came through that 2000 Japs were gathered in the village of Bawgaligyi and in bashas to the S.W. En route our six aircraft were recalled owing to bad weather reported over the target area.
29th	The Adjutant returned from Calcutta with crockery for the mess.
30th	Everyone busy packing up in preparation for our move to Meiktila.

July 1945

Operations.

During April, May and June a slightly chaotic state was caused by weather, change of location and the conversion from Hurricanes to Thunderbolts. That does not sound at all impressive, in fact the bare details are definitely dull, but behind those dry particulars, and I don't mean the weather, the stage was being set for something new. In July the players knew their parts, they were equipped for a public appearance and shortly the Japs would be aware of a show that was going to be a big hit. I refer, of course to the conversion, the new era of 34 Squadron who had operated against the Japs on Blenheims and Hurries from the days of Singapore.

A pilot likes his aircraft, to him it is the perfect aircraft, and one does not change one's battle office with as little concern as changing a pair of trousers. The Hurricane was the figurehead of innumerable tales of aerial success and tradition, but the Thunderbolt came as a stranger. Different habits and an accent as unlike the hum of a Merlin as the two Nations who use it.

The P.47 was designed as a high level patrol fighter and an escort for the Fortresses and Liberators of the U.S. Bombardment Group. With its Turbo supercharger it is eminently suited to such duties, but near the ground it is rather like making a fast swimmer race in treacle. No one will deny it is operating in a secondary capacity, but I challenge anyone to say it is not achieving first rate results.

The pilots accepted this newcomer without prejudice and it has not let them down. Nine new members were direct from C.T.U. where they had chosen Thunderbolt in preference to the Spitfire. Their reasons were sound. A radial engine is immune from the problems confronting a liquid-cooled motor in hot climates and with its long range it could make the most of weather where monsoon conditions often hampered operations. As the U.S.A.A.F. had shown during the fight in Europe where almost all single engine aircraft had come down to low level activity, it was a useful weapon for bombing and strafing. Jokes were made by the fellows training on Spits., "Evasion action in a T'Bolt is taken by undoing your straps and running round the cockpit" they used to say. But the chaps were confident and keen about operating in the Flying Battleship. Those of the pilots who had converted were quick to appreciate its qualities and the Wolf pack showed its fangs.

Operating from Meiktila a bomb load was possible, and 34, proud of its close support to the Army were ready to take on any target and blast the Japs to the land of their ancestors.

No finer opportunity could be desired than the mass attempt of the enemy to escape during July. Targets were good and on the nursery slopes of the Pegu Yomas and the Sittang Valley, where opposition was slight, the pilots learnt how to lay their bombs bang on the target, and brought their standard of air to ground firing up to such a pitch of perfection that each pilot knew when a tightening of the finger would send a gush of ·5 into a foxhole or suspicious looking basha. When the time comes for the next campaign 34 will look forward to as much action as they can get, and if we are fortunate enough to be in at the kill when Singapore is deloused we shall feel thoroughly happy to fly in the same skies as the Blenheims who first formed our Squadron.

The following is a general outline of the situation of Military Operations which go hand in hand with the work done by this Squadron in July, and which is considered the last phase in Burma.

Split by the rapid thrust our armies made from Mandalay to Rangoon, the Japs lost any strategic advantage they may have held. Left to them were the tactics of escape. While Victory Parades were taking place in Rangoon many thousands of Japs lay up in the Pegu Yomas, and others fought a rearguard action along such routes as the Mawchi Road. Obviously, this isolated Jap Army would need supplies, and more plain was the fact that they could not get them. Come July and they were massed for a break-through. From Toungoo South they started to filter across heading for the Sittang where it was a case of "Cross or Die". Weakened by disease and shortage of food they were given four pieces of bamboo with which to float themselves across the river. They had a few handfuls of rice and a small amount of ammunition. Pretty desperate measures.

From Mokpalin, East of the Sittang, they attempted to form a bridgehead, and spreading out in the swampy paddy they tried to push a wedge into our lines to help their retreating forces making for a temporary respite in the Moulmein area. Deprived of mountain cover and the low cloud which had kept them covered and safe from the air, they stepped into the Valley and slaughter commenced. By the end of the first week they knew what it would cost them but they continued. They had to.

21/7/45

One afternoon 34 Squadron were at readiness and frequent showers made a job seem unlikely. Some thought it was a joke when the A.L.O. told them to report for immediate briefing, the strip was considered u/s. But the break through had started with a rush and the Army had targets for us. A message was sent to the Group Captain for his decision for a take off on the soaking strip, and by the time briefing was over permission had been granted. A terrific atmosphere had been built up in a few minutes. It would be a gamble, but had they not been allowed to take the air disappointment would have been great. The chaps boarded their transport and went off yelling the familiar slogan of 34, "Push on regardless". The scramble was complete and the form-up was an achievement in itself. Low cloud and local storms made the task of seeing the aircraft ahead a tricky business, but they did it and the next Flight, as they started their engines, saw them disappear into the one blue gap which threw open the course for Pyu.

They arrived to receive instructions from V.C.P. Chico. He was issuing targets like jam tarts at a Sunday School outing and the air was full of various callsigns, map references and once or twice the sound of machine-gun fire as a pilot spoke to his Section as he strafed. 34 took on a village and left it in ruins. As they set course for Base other Flights of Spits and T'Bolts could be seen belting down on targets. One aircraft alone killed 150 Japs out of a group sighted in open ground.

Weather had closed in North of Toungoo and the pilots stayed there the night. From the strip, 37's were pounding the enemy 8 miles away and one could feel the atmosphere of war which at Meiktila seemed so far away. Throughout the night small parties of Japs were prowling around the town, presumably raiding to obtain food and spasmodic bursts of gunfire and the explosion of grenades continued till early morning.

Prized among Squadrons is the award of a "Strawberry", the honour given by the Army for an especially good show. In July there was a general "Strawberry" shared by 34, but here is how they got one for themselves alone.

3/7/45

East of Pyu a concentration of Japs were reported and our own patrols who had the village under observation from behind the enemy lines would give a signal if it was worthy of attack. The formation arrived and the signal was given. A puff of smoke and the aircraft formed their circle. Gunsights on bomb switches set to "fuse and select". Often a village looks deserted and one wonders if there is a living thing in the clustered bashas and surrounding trees. This looked no different. The bombs were well placed throughout its length, and guns poured bullets over the entire area. A couple of days later the report came through and the amount of Jap dead found when our troops walked in was around the 300 mark. That kind of thing is very satisfying.

Occasions when the Jap is seen are rare. July gives four instances. "Trombone", the V.C.P. of Nyaungkashe, once directed sections of a Flight to search for gun positions. Jap 75's had been active after dark and on one night they cased 25 casualties. Having bombed a clump of trees the No.2 of a section was almost on the point of pulling out from his last strafing run when a figure darted across in front of him. A quick squirt and the Jap was in the middle of a bullet group. At the same time a small railway station at Laya had been attacked and lining the embankment were dug-in positions. Abreast of him one pilot could see Japs crouching, and swinging round in a tight turn he hosed them with his guns. Some fled for a safer spot but it did them no good. As soon as their movement betrayed them, they were cut down. On another job, 34 were bombing a village bordered by a Chaung and as they arrived 6 or 7 figures were seen leaving the village by Sampan. They dived over the side as the attack commenced and disappeared. For ever we hope. Lastly on another bombing job a figure was seen hunched up in a trench. There is no doubt that he was well perforated.

Later in the month Nyaungkashe was taken by the Japs, but in the opinion of an A.L.O. it hardly mattered as the more they exposed themselves the quicker we could kill them.

9/7/45

Abortive operations are bound to occur, but not shown on the sortie report or known to anyone but the pilots concerned is the degree of attempt which was made before the monsoon won the argument. Here is an example of such an operation.

Two Flights took off early in an attempt to reach respectively, the Lower Sittang area and an enemy troop concentration West of Toungoo. If those going to the Sittang target were held up by weather they would return and attack the target assigned to the second Flight in the foothills. For quite a distance the forward Flight could be seen spread out some three miles away. Small black dots against the sky. Over the R/T we could hear them commenting on the cloud, and they passed information back to us. They were going through a gap and suggested we might try the same way. Closing the formation, we wriggled through and stooged along between layers. At this stage one of the No. 2's in the first Flight fell too far behind his No. 1 and became separated from the Formation. It cost him his life. As was his duty, the No. 1 remained to try and contact the missing pilot, the other three got through and bombed the target.

Dash and discretion are wisely tempered but no pilot of 34 who realises his obligation to the Army, and all of them do, will be satisfied unless he knows it was absolutely impossible to penetrate the weather. The groundcrews take pride in their Squadron when it comes back without its bombs and other Squadrons on the same day return with loaded racks.

"Push on regardless".

The road to Mawchi is a difficult one for the Army. Low cloud prevents regular air support, the roads impede transport and the Jap lingers in the jungle. To displace him is not easy.

17/7/45

However, there were times such as the 17th of July when 34 were able to put a Flight over the mountains. The brown jobs were being held up by Jap cross fire where the muddy road straightened to cross a chaung. The bomb-line was 400 yards form our target and mortar smoke showed us where the enemy were. Bombs tore gaps in the jungle and strafing-runs sprayed the dense cover. We hope it helped the Army.

Actual figures for the month's operations are as follows:

Operational Sorties	214
Operational Flying Hours	602·09
Bombs Dropped	344 × 500
Ammunition Expended	198,434 × ·5

Meiktila (Burma)

Squadron Movements.

Acting on instructions from H.Q. 221 Group, the Unit moved from Kinmagan to Meiktila on the 1st July 1945. The move was made in two parts.

(a) The Air Party, consisting of the Squadron aircraft and

(b) the Road Party, consisting of the ground officers and airmen. No 7034 Servicing Echelon also moved to Meiktila, that move being spread over several days and being accomplished by road and rail. Both moves were carried out according to plan and no difficulties were encountered.

Postings. Whilst at Meiktila, the Squadron will be administered by H.Q. 910 Wing.
No postings were effected during the month.

Casualties. 1801115 F/Sgt Neate R.S. (Pilot) killed as the result of a flying accident on 9th July 1945.
1603065 F/Sgt Murray D.S. (Pilot) killed as the result of a flying accident on 12th July 1945.
187718 P/O L. Soulsby (Pilot) Missing – particulars unknown as the result of a flying accident on 17th June 1945 (this information only just received).

Medical. The Officer in Medical Charge (F/Lt Inglis) reports: "During the month there were no straightforward cases of malaria, but it is interesting to note that three patients admitted to hospital, one with Bacillary Dysentery two with Hepatitis, were found to have M.T. parasites in the blood. These patients were on Mepacrine, one tablet daily, and yet the parasite which is most influenced by mepacrine was still in circulation and malaria symptoms developed whilst in hospital.

It would seem therefore that mepacrine is merely suppressive and does not keep the body free from Plasmodium, and that any upset of the normal metabolism will precipitate an attack. Under these circumstances, the present disciplinary measures in connection with malaria would appear to be unjustified.

As mepacrine is only suppressive, the question of treatment on leaving malarious areas arises. The instructions in Acsea (Admin) Order 51/45 advise continuing one tablet daily for 28 days after leaving the area, and Medical Administrative Instructions advise Blanket Treatment. In view of the present findings, it seems that the latter is the proper course to adopt.

With the control of the fly population by D.D.T. bacillary dysentery has disappeared; there was only one case during the month.

During the month there were five cases of Infective Hepatitis, but only in one instance was it possible to trace the connection between cases."

August 1945

Meiktila (Burma)

The month started off very badly. On the first operation of the month 6 aircraft set out to attack Japanese positions on the railway embankment near Abya. Unfortunately, the weather prevented them from reaching their target, nor was it possible to make the alternative target, a body of some 200 Japs in the village of Tinugyung. A second flight of 6 aircraft also went out on a similar job, but on receiving an adverse weather report en route, returned to base without accomplishing their mission.

The weather improved on the third, and 12 aircraft were able to make a successful sortie. Although briefed to bomb and strafe Nyaungkashe, the a/c were diverted by the V.C.P. "Pinetar" to Satthwagon. 'A' Flight took the southern end of the village and put all its bombs (with the exception of one hang up) in the target area. Subsequent strafing runs produced 2 large fires. 'B' Flight attacked the Paungyi Kyaung and obtained a heavy concentration on the target and started a fire on strafing.

On the following day, the fourth, another neat attack was made on dug in positions at Nyaungkashe, 'A' Flight observed slit trenches on top of the embankment at either side of the railway track and 10 bombs were dropped on these. Bashas in the neighbourhood were then strafed with unobserved results. 'B' Flight went for dug-in positions to the North of the railway bridge and did some very accurate bombing. Pilots were of the opinion that all but four of the trenches had been destroyed. This Flight also strafed bashas in the neighbourhood but again no results were seen.

On the fifth, sixth and seventh of the month, the monsoon had us in its grip and no operations were possible, but an early start on the eighth enabled us to go out to Taangalon where a very good attack was made by 12 aircraft resulting in extensive damage and several bashas left smouldering. We were not to know this at the time, but this was the last offensive action taken by 34 Squadron in the Japanese campaign. The honour of dropping the last 2 bombs fell to Sgt. Littlewood.

On the tenth of the month vague news was heard over the wireless to the effect that the total capitulation of the Japanese was to be expected any moment. In spite of this however, the war still seemed to be carrying on and the Army had several jobs for us to do on the days following.

Unfortunately, the weather on the tenth and eleventh was very bad and permitted no flying whatsoever (this was, perhaps, a good job because after our rather premature victory celebrations no one felt inclined to do any serious work). On the twelfth of August, 12 a/c went out in support of the Army but because of heavy storms encountered en route they had to call the job off and returned to base.

Zayatkwin.

By now it had become very apparent that the war really was coming to an end. No more offensive operations were carried out, but all aircraft were standing by with bombs "just in case". During this period the Squadron moved South to Zayatkwin. The final surrender of the Japanese having been negotiated, we took upon ourselves a new role, that of dropping leaflets. These were of various types according to whether they were intended for the local inhabitants of Jap occupied areas, isolated groups of the enemy who had received no official notification of the news of the surrender, or the guards of Jap P.O.W. Camps. After operations the pilots found these sorties very tame and, in some cases, where long distances were involved, rather uncomfortable. One such of these, a leaflet drop on Kra Buri on the extreme southern tip of Burma, involved a round trip of over 1,000 miles and five and a half hours flying. There is nothing very much that can be said about these operations because of their routine nature. A fair number were rendered abortive by very bad weather conditions but the remainder were highly successful. In many cases both the Japs and the local inhabitants were seen to be eagerly reading the leaflets and there is no doubt that they caused some excitement. The very last of these trips in August, on the 30th, resulted in a casualty. Warrant Officer G.E. Chaney and F/Lt Williamson had reached Kra Buri and were just about to drop their containers when the former called up over the R.T. and said that he was having trouble with his aircraft. Nothing more was seen or heard of him, but on searching the area F/Lt. Williamson saw what he took to be the remains of an aircraft burning on the ground. No further details of this casualty are yet known.

So ends the month of August, a notable one in many a man's life but not particularly interesting for 34 Squadron. Operational Summary:

Total Operational Sorties	85
Total Operational Hours	206·35
Total Bombs Dropped	72 × 500lb. 22 leaflet bombs
Total Ammunition Expended	48,520 × ·5

Administration – Movements.

On the 18th August, 1945, the Squadron moved from Meiktila to Zayatkwin there coming under the Administrative and Operational Control of Headquarters 909 Wing. The move was carried out in two parts (a) the first party consisting of the Squadron aircraft, and (b) the second party consisting of the Squadron ground crews and those of its Servicing Echelon

Personnel.

who travelled by transport aircraft. The move was carried out according to plan and no snags were encountered.

The following postings were effected during the month:

F/O R.H. Williams (146913) Pilot to 42 Squadron.

Eight Hurricane trained pilots previously shown on attachment to 229 Group were posted to that Headquarters for flying duties.

One casualty occurred in August: 1318357 W/O G.E. Chaney, Pilot, missing as a result of a flying accident on 30/8/45.

Medical.

The Officer in Medical Charge (F/Lt Inglis) reports "the new camp sites at Zayatkwin were flooded on arrival and tentage, bedding, and clothes were soon wet. Despite this the sickness incidence has not risen appreciably and the general health of the Squadron remains as it was. There have been no cases of outstanding clinical interest during the month.

September 1945

Zayatkwin

We continued our new role of operations, and on the morning of the 1st September, sorties were flown dropping leaflet bombs on Mokpalin, Thaton, Bilin, Kyaikto and Moulmein. A further two sorties were flown in the afternoon and the areas of Chaungwa and Satchaung were successfully covered by the leaflet bombs. In Moulmein, large crowds were seen gathering and reading the pamphlets.

The weather again prevented operations on the 2nd, and 3rd. Repeated attempts to get through were made each day from 4th to 9th, to recce Prisoner of War Camps in Thani and Thaton areas, but despite the determined efforts of all concerned, the weather had the last word and all sorties were abortive.

On the morning of the 10th the weather had improved considerably, so with light hearts two pilots took off to recce P.O.W. Camps at Capienmai, Lum-Sum, Zai-Yok and Yah-Takua. Unfortunately, one of the aircraft developed a fault in the petrol system, so both aircraft returned to base.

A further two sorties were flown to P.O.W. Camps at Thani and despite a deterioration of weather conditions, the camp was successfully located. The pilots saw some of the men in the camp compound playing games, but these soon ceased and the players began waving to the aircraft. This was a welcome sight to the pilot and they returned happy in the knowledge that they had inspired a measure of hope in their less fortunate comrades in the camp.

Next day, 11th, two aircraft set off to recce camps at Mergui and Ross Is. Over Tavoy Point a terrific storm was raging, so they climbed through a gap in the clouds and continued on course for Mergui. Shortly afterwards, one of the aircraft, piloted by F/Sgt Butler, D.E., was seen to enter cloud. No message was heard over the R.T. and although F/O Mason, who was leading the Section, called up repeatedly and searched the area for over half an hour, nothing further was seen or heard of the missing aircraft, so he returned to base.

P.O.W. Camp along the Moulmein-Bangkok Rly. and camps in the Chienmai, Tum-Sum, Zai-Yok, Tah-Takua area were successfully pin-pointed, but all the camps appeared deserted indicating that the occupants had already been evacuated safely. So ended our operational activities which seemed rather tame compared to our tasks of the proceeding months, but nevertheless very necessary.

Operational Summary:

Total Operational Sorties	35
Total Operational Hours	66·10
Total Bombs Dropped	7 leaflet bombs
Total Ammunition Expended	Nil

Personnel. The following postings were effected during the month.

F/O C.J. Tedder (163200) Pilot, to 131 R. & S.U.

P/O A.C. Findon (190831), to 42 Squadron.

F/O R.R. Leng (177220) Adjt. To 85 A.S.P.

Notification has also been received that S/Ldr G.T.A. Douglas (at present on compassionate leave), is to proceed on posting to command No. 28 Squadron, and F/Lt D.L. Williamson (Acting Squadron Commander) to R.A.F. Station, Peshawar.

One casualty occurred during the month. 1615752 F/Sgt Butler, D., missing as a result of a Flying Accident on 10/9/45.

Medical. The Squadron Medical officer (F/Lt A. Inglis) reports the following: "The Sick parades have shewn a slight increase this month, the average daily sick being four. This is accounted for by the number of cases of Otitis Externa which required daily treatment and so add to the normal numbers on the Sick Report. The end of the monsoon should reduce the number of ear complaints.

After the departure of 909 Wing, there was a shortage of Grade III Paraffin for the preparation of D.D.T. Spraying was in abeyance for about fourteen days but there was no appreciable increase in the fly population and there have been no cases of dysentery.

Supplies of D.D.T. are now available but the quantity is insufficient for large scale spraying operations, so that the mosquito still remains our most troublesome pest.

Supplies of clothing, particularly boots, have been difficult to obtain and many men are to be seen in unserviceable boots. Some individuals have solved the problem at their own expense by buying boots from the Burmese who charge 10 to 15 Rupees a pair.

Appendix II

Extract From No.34 Squadron Operations Record Book – Record of Events Relating to Angus Findon's Sorties, July to August 1945

Date	Aircraft	¹Crew	Duty	Up	Down
5/7/45	KL261	F/Sgt Dawkin	Ops.	0630.	1000.
	KL398	P/O Findon	Ops.	0630.	1000.
	KL311	F/Sgt Hopkinson	Ops.	0630.	1000.
	KJ274	P/O Tedder	Ops.	0630.	1000.
	Details	The section arrived to find "Trombone" operating again and two a/c were sent to bomb and strafe LAYA Railway Station, QG2042. Four bombs were dropped in the attack but three falling on the station did not exploded and the remaining one kipped to the South and blew up in open ground. A number of Japs dug in along the Railway embankment were strafed 3 times, many strikes being scored. The other two a/c made a dummy run to locate camouflaged gun positions in area of QG358190. A clump of trees seemed a likely position and became the target for 4 bombs. Two exploded among the trees, wrecking them completely and two, which undershot to the North were not seen to explode. In the last of 3 strafing-runs Japs were seen running for cover of the newly-formed bomb craters. A further two runs were made and the area was well covered.			
6/7/45	KL241	S/L Douglas	Ops.	1207.	1355.
	KJ252	W/O Perry	Ops.	1207.	1450.
	KL200	F/Sgt Marr	Ops.	1207.	1450.
	KL281	W/O Usmar	Ops.	1207.	1450.
	KL328	W/O Auton	Ops.	1207.	1450.
	KL189	F/Sgt Bliss	Ops.	1207.	1450.
	KL261	F/O Williams	Ops.	1207.	1450.
	KL311	F/O Sorrell	Ops.	1207.	1450.
	KL201	P/O Findon	Ops.	1207.	1450.

---

1. All Thunderbolt II.

Date	Aircraft	Crew	Duty	Up	Down
	Details	Cabrank requested for V.C.P. "Trombone" over NYAUNGKASHE. Attempts were made to penetrate heavy cloud at deck level north of the target. Weather deteriorated rapidly and mission was abandoned/ A/c KL241 landed at TOUNGOO at 1355 with Engine trouble.			
9/7/45	KL281	F/O Williams	Ops.	0800.	0950.
	KL218	F/O Mason	Ops.	0800.	0950.
	KL261	F/Sgt Dawkin	Ops.	0800.	0950.
	KJ356	F/Sgt Bliss	Ops.	0800.	0950.
	KL328	P/O Findon	Ops.	0800.	0950.
	Details	In valley S.W. of TOUNGOO 500 Japs were due to be bombed and strafed but weather intervened and the mission was abandoned.			
17/7/45	KL189	F/L Williamson	Ops.	1350.	1600.
	KJ356	F/Sgt Holloway	Ops.	1350.	1600.
	KL219	W/O Auton	Ops.	1350.	1600.
	KL241	F/Sgt Bliss	Ops.	1350.	1600.
	KL261	F/O Williams	Ops.	1350.	1600.
	KL201	P/O Findon	Ops.	1350.	1600.
	Details	Japanese positions, on a bend in the MAWCHI Road at QB204939, were holding up own troops who were compelled to cross open ground and a chaung. Weather in the target area was excellent and smoke laid by artillery indicated the enemy's position. Dense Jungle prevented the observation of any details but the bombs all fell in the spot marked causing good explosions, one of which was followed by thick grey smoke. The Jungle was well sprayed in six strafing-runs.			
21/7/45	KL189	F/L Williamson	Ops.	1505.	1815.
	KL201	P/O Findon	Ops.	1505.	1815.
	KL241	F/Sgt Dawkin	Ops.	1505.	1815.
	KL261	F/Sgt Bliss	Ops.	1505.	1815.
	KL328	F/O Mason	Ops.	1505.	1815.
	KJ356	W/O Chaney	Ops.	1505.	1815.
	Details	In Cabrank order, the first Flight arrived to be directed by V.C.P. "Chico". Given the village of TAGUNGAING, QA946341, the a/c laid their bombs in positions which thoroughly wrecked the village and then went in to strafe it twice. Weather closed in toward Base and the Flight returned to land at TOUNGOO. Brake failure on one a/c caused it to leave the runway and sustain slight damage in a nose-over on soft ground. The pilot was unhurt.			

Appendix II   113

Date	Aircraft	Crew	Duty	Up	Down
22/7/45	KL189	F/L Williamson	Local.	1320.	1415.
	KL201	P/O Findon	Local.	1320.	1415.
	KL261	F/Sgt Bliss	Local.	1320.	1415.
	KL328	F/O Mason	Local.	1320.	1415.
	KL356	W/O Chaney	Local.	1320.	1415.
	Details	TOUNGOO to BASE.			
24/7/45	KL261	F/L Williamson	Ops.	1540.	1810.
	KJ356	F/Sgt Palmer	Ops.	1540.	1810.
	KL328	F/O Mason	Ops.	1540.	1810.
	KJ282	Sgt Thwaits	Ops.	1540.	1810.
	KL219	W/O Auton	Ops.	1540.	1810.
	KL311	F/Sgt Dawkin	Ops.	1540.	1810.
	KL201	P/O Findon	Ops.	1540.	1810.
	KJ332	F/Sgt Marr	Ops.	1540.	1810.
	KJ274	F/Sgt Hopkinson	Ops.	1550.	1820.
	KL250	Sgt Sheehan	Ops.	1550.	1820.
	KL244	F/O Tedder	Ops.	1550.	1820.
	KJ282	W/O Usmar	Ops.	1550.	1820.
	Details	Japanese concentrations in the West half of WEGYI, from QB014495 to 010489, were bombed and strafed. "A" Flight arrived punctually at given T.O.T. and smoke indication was given as first a/c commenced bombing dive. Pilots were instructed to precision bomb various sectors and the desired results were achieved. Four bombs failed to explode but the remainder caused sufficient destruction to make up for this. The following four strafing-runs are known to have affected the majority of the bashas but, unfortunately, no fires were caused due to dampness. "B" Flight closely followed the last attack and placed their 12 bombs along the line by the results of "A" Flight's attacks. Two strafing-runs were made but it was impossible to see much on account of trees.			
28/7/45	KL332	F/L Williamson	Ops.	1230.	1530.
	KL281	F/Sgt Hornsey	Ops.	1230.	1530.
	KL356	F/O Mason	Ops.	1230.	1530.
	KJ220	W/O Holloway	Ops.	1230.	1530.
	KL219	W/O Auton	Ops.	1230.	1530.
	KL201	P/O Findon	Ops.	1230.	1530.
	Details	Jap troops were reported to be dug in at the West end of KYAUKSAUNG, QB092395, QB992393, suspected positions were to be strafed on the bund and South bank of the river extending to LETPADAN.			

Date	Aircraft	Crew	Duty	Up	Down

Twelve miles East of PYU, the target was seen as a long narrow village with many bashas. The greatest concentration of these was at the West end and this was the target for 12 bombs. Two bombs failed to explode but 6 which fell among the bashas caused heavy damage and 4 direct hits on a KG destroyed and damaged adjacent out-buildings. As the Leader pulled out from his bombing attack, he noticed 6 or 7 troops crossing the river in a small boat. He ordered his No.2 to give this target a burst as he bombed but before this was possible the boat had been lost to sight. Three strafing-runs completed the operation and these produced a large fire. A pilot of another squadron, which was in the area earlier in the day, reported a tank in MINLAN-TZEIK, QB366901, and this was searched for accordingly. However nothing was seen and dense jungle in this particular locality rendered observation extremely difficult.

30/7/45	KL189	F/L Williamson	Ops.	0740.	1030.
	KL356	F/O Mason	Ops.	0740.	1030.
	KL281	W/O Chaney	Ops.	0740.	1030.
	KL219	F/Sgt Dawkin	Ops.	0740.	1030.
	KL201	P/O Findon	Ops.	0740.	1030.
	Details				

The Flight circled beneath low cloud while waiting for the other formation to complete their job on a nearby target. During this time own troops were seen advancing in force East of the SITTANG, and form of greeting was exchanged between one pilot and those on the ground who waved vigorously and appeared to take an extremely good view of their Air Support. After orbiting for about five mins., the air was clear and the Flight proceeded to their target. This was a compact village, heavily wooded named MYETYE, QB198268. Two bombs in the middle failed to explode but the remainder caused much damage to bashas. In strafing-runs a fire was started which was obviously not a basha, as the thick white smoke was of an uncommon type.

30/7/45	KL311	F/L Williamson	Ops.	1325.	1640.
	KL189	F/Sgt Hopkinson	Ops.	1325.	1640.
	KJ282	Sgt Soper	Ops.	1325.	1640.
	KL250	F/Sgt Dark	Ops.	1325.	1640.

Appendix II 115

Date	Aircraft	Crew	Duty	Up	Down
	KL219	F/Sgt Dawkin	Ops.	1325.	1640.
	KL201	P/O Findon	Ops.	1325.	1640.
	KL356	F/O Mason	Ops.	1325.	1640.
	KL281	W/O Chaney	Ops.	1325.	1640.

Details The formation arrived over the target which was easily recognised as a fairly long village running N to S. The Japanese had been putting up a strong resistance against own troops, who were halted in their advance 200 yds. East of the village. When the Flight arrived, shelling was in progress by our own artillery and V.C.P. "Pinetar" was contacted and informed of our readiness for immediate Air Support. The V.C.P. called off his guns and mentioned that previously attacking a/c had met with return fire. The Southern end of the village was the target for sixteen bombs and this half of SATHWAGYON, QG311220-310224, received a heavy pounding. All bombs were in the target area and one very satisfactory explosion which may have been an ammo. dump sent a column of smoke, mixed with red flame, to a height of 150ft. Five strafing-runs covered every position of possible cover.

Date	Aircraft	Crew	Duty	Up	Down
3/8/45	KL189	F/L Williamson	Ops.	1440.	1755.
	KJ328	P/O Findon	Ops.	1440.	1755.
	KL218	F/Sgt Dawkin	Ops.	1440.	1755.
	KL281	W/O Holloway	Ops.	1440.	1755.
	KL219	W/O Auton	Ops.	1440.	1755.
	KJ332	F/Sgt Palmer	Ops.	1440.	1755.
	KL311	F/O Williams	Ops.	1500.	1815.
	KL840	F/O Tedder	Ops.	1500.	1815.
	KL200	F/Sgt Marr	Ops.	1500.	1815.
	KJ252	W/O Usmar	Ops.	1500.	1815.
	KJ272	F/Sgt Hopkinson	Ops.	1500.	1815.
	KL183	F/Sgt Dark	Ops.	1500.	1815.

Details Briefed to bomb and strafe NYAUNGKASHE. A/c were diverted to SATTHWAGON on instructions from V.C.P. "Pinetar". Taking the southern end of the village, "A" Flight put all its bombs in the target area with the exception of one which hung up and fell without exploding in a paddy field. In succeeding strafing runs, two large fires were caused. "B" Flight went into attack the paungyi kyaung. The result of

Date	Aircraft	Crew	Duty	Up	Down
		this was a heavy concentration in the target area and strafing runs caused another fire.			
4/8/45	KL189	F/L Williamson	Ops.	1125.	1425.
	KL281	F/Sgt Thwaits	Ops.	1125.	1425.
	KL219	W/O Auton	Ops.	1125.	1425.
	KL270	F/Sgt Bliss	Ops.	1125.	1425.
	KJ328	P/O Findon	Ops.	1125.	1425.
	KL218	W/O Holloway	Ops.	1125.	1425.
	KL311	F/O Williams	Ops.	1135.	1445.
	KL840	F/Sgt Butler	Ops.	1135.	1445.
	KL200	F/Sgt Marr	Ops.	1135.	1445.
	KJ252	F/Sgt Sheehan	Ops.	1135.	1445.
	KJ272	F/Sgt Hopkinson	Ops.	1135.	1445.
	KL183	Sgt Soper	Ops.	1135.	1445.
	Details	Jap dug in positions, 200 yards either side of a railway bridge, North of NYAUNGKASHE, QG32221, were to be bombed, while bashas on the outskirts of the town, at QG322169, were to be strafed. "A" Flight observed slit trenches on the top of the embankment either side of the track, and 10 bombs fell on this target. Two which failed to explode were seen to fall at the North end of the bridge. A/c then visited the bashas and delivered an attack with unobserved results. "B" Flight took on dug in positions, 150 yards North of the bridge, and very accurate bombing gave rise to the estimate that all but 4 of the trenches had been affected. Bashas at QG324170 were then attacked in five strafing runs.			
12/8/45	KL189	F/L Williamson	Ops.	1550.	1610.
	KL281	F/Sgt Thwaits	Ops.	1550.	1610.
	KJ328	F/O Mason	Ops.	1550.	1610.
	KJ356	W/O Holloway	Ops.	1550.	1610.
	KL201	P/O Findon	Ops.	1550.	1610.
	KL281	W/O Chaney	Ops.	1550.	1610.
	Details	Heavy storms encountered South of PYINMANA, prevented a/c from proceeding to target at YELI KAYINYWA, QB183204.			
18/8/45	KL189	F/L Williamson	Local	1500.	1655.
	KL281	F/Sgt Thwaits	Local	1500.	1655.
	KJ328	F/O Mason	Local	1500.	1655.
	KJ356	W/O Holloway	Local	1500.	1655.
	KL201	P/O Findon	Local	1500.	1655.

Date	Aircraft	Crew	Duty	Up	Down
	KL281	W/O Chaney	Local	1500.	1655.
	Details	MEIKTILA to ZAYATKWIN.			
28/8/45	KJ328	F/Sgt Dawkin	Ops.	0650.	0845.
	KL183	P/O Findon	Ops.	0650.	0845.
	Details	Village of KADAINGTI, 87 miles East of Base, was located in the hills. Several attempts were made from various directions and eventually the mission was abandoned, due to zero visibility ten miles from the target.			
29/8/45	KL200	F/Sgt Dawkin	Ops.	0800.	0900.
	KJ356	P/O Findon	Ops.	0800.	0900.
	Details	A/c set course for KRA BURI but faulty long-range tanks forced them to return.			
29/8/45	KL270	F/Sgt Dawkin	Ops.	1605.	1800.
	KL219	P/O Findon	Ops.	1605.	1800.
	Details	Town of THAYZAYASTI was found at cross-roads South of MOULMEIN. Leaflets completely covered streets and houses and both Jap and local villagers were seen to be reading them. 6 miles North of the town, an overcrowded trainload of Jap troops was seen heading south.			

Appendix III

Extract from Air Chief Marshal Park's Despatch on Air Operations in South-East Asia, 3 May 1945 to 12 September 1945: The Battle of the Sittang Bend

In an attempt to create a large scale diversion of the Allied ground forces, the Japanese, at the opening of July, launched an offensive at the Sittang from the bridgehead which they tenaciously held on the right bank opposite Mokpalin. It was flat, open country with scattered scrub, and some very fierce fighting took place in appalling weather at Nyaungkashe, Abya, and Myikye. The village of Nyaungkashe, indeed, changed hands several times.

Air support thrown in by 221 Group, included the Spitfire and Thunderbolt squadrons operating continuous patrols or 'Cabranks' in the Nyaungkashe area. The enemy took exceedingly heavy punishment. His determination to hold this area, at all costs, however, until the large Japanese forces to the north got down past Bilin, with the strategic town of Mokpalin on their right, safeguarded by the Sittang troops, was obvious.

Day after day, gun positions, troop concentrations, and river craft of all descriptions were subjected to intensive attacks by the air forces, bringing sincere thanks from the Army. On July 4th, No. 42 Squadron's Thunderbolts had a most successful day, when a 105mm gun was wrecked and two other guns silenced at Nyaungkashe.

It was at this time that some forces of 7 Indian Infantry Division found themselves in a precarious position as a result of the determined Japanese thrust, but, assisted by air attack, succeeded in extricating themselves.

'With the help of excellent air support quickly given,' wrote Lieutenant General Messervy to Air Vice-Marshal Bouchier, A.O.C. 221 Group, 'I have been able to extricate some four hundred men, including sixty wounded, from a difficult situation with good knocks to the Japs at the same time.'

It was noted throughout these air operations, and further substantiated by ground reports, that a considerable number of Japanese troops were killed as a result of air attacks.

By July 11th, the Japanese offensive at the Sittang Bend had been contained, though the enemy still retained their foothold on the right bank of the Sittang, opposite Mokpalin.

Air Power Assists the Guerrillas.
As the month advanced, a notable movement of enemy troops endeavouring to cross the Sittang River in parties at various points between Shwegyin and Kyaukke, kept the Spitfire squadrons on continuous patrol over the Sittang River exceedingly active. Thunderbolt squadrons, too, came down from the Meiktila area to attack forces of Japanese numbering, in some instances, one thousand strong, as they made their way eastwards. The large scale break-through from the Pegu Yomas had not yet started.

It was in this area of the Sittang, and also in the east, on the right bank of the Salween, that the organised guerrillas, which had been brought under the control of 12th Army, ambushed hundreds of escaping Japanese troops moving down from Loikaw to Papun, and literally massacred them. No enemy party was safe from these guerrillas under Force 136 who, with portable W/T, kept base informed of the enemy's movements and as a result provided the Mosquitos and Spitfires with definite targets, which they bombed and strafed untiringly.

The guerrillas' flag was seen regularly by pilots heading for their targets. They were assisted by large indicator arrows on the ground, and even cryptic messages which the levies had conceived. On one occasion, pilots, correctly interpreting a message, 'In M', located a Japanese force in a marsh.

Following a heavy raid on Pa-An, one of the principal staging villages used by the Japanese while moving down the Salween valley, a message sent from our land forces to 273 and 607 Squadrons on July 1st said:-

More than five hundred Japs killed in last heavy raid on Pa-An. Did not tell you before as awaiting confirmation. Congrats to pilots.

An earlier report had described this whole area after the raids as covered in dust and smoke, with Japanese soldiers seen running about in panic and rushing for shelter as aircraft came down to strafe them. The Mosquito Squadrons got equally effective results for, during a strike at Kawludo, an enemy staging post in the Salween valley, north of Papun, a ground report stated that over one hundred Japanese troops had been killed.

Thunderbolts and Spitfires carried out a very successful attack on July 15th and 16th, in the Shwegyin Chaung area of the Sittang, and a message from Kyadwin to 113 Squadron and 607 Squadron said:-'Tell R.A.F. strike great success.'

North East of Kyadwin, at Paungzeik, Mosquitos of 47 Squadron, on July 16th, made a bombing and strafing attack in the Paungzeik valley and 51 dead Japanese were counted after the attack. Yet another attack by aircraft on the 19th, at Shanywathit, resulted in two direct hits being made on a house which was full of Japanese troops, and over eighty are believed to have been killed.

The reports of successful air strikes against the escaping enemy were many and varied. In the credit for their success the guerrillas of Force 136 must equally share. Their daring in approaching large enemy parties and making sudden furious assaults on them with gunfire and grenades before retiring to their hideouts to plan further surprise raids, was outstanding in this final killing of the Japanese in Burma. The risks, too, which they ran, while blatantly guiding aircraft on to enemy concentrations, frequently involved them in hazardous escapes. Many escapes were only made possible indeed, by aircraft swooping in between the levies and the enemy, strafing the Japanese pursuers. If caught, guerrillas were tortured cruelly by the enemy.

Tribute to R.A.F. from Guerrilla Leader.
A tribute paid to the Royal Air Force in Burma came from the leader of one of these courageous parties operating in the Okpyat area of the Sittang: 'Both I and every guerrilla would like to make it known to every pilot who took part in the battle of the Okpyat area just how much all the brilliant offensive action of the R.A.F. fighter-bomber pilots was appreciated,' wrote Captain J. Waller, British Officer in charge of Force 136 Guerrillas, Okpyat. 'From our point of view on the ground, we wished that we had more air ground strips so that we could write in full – Hats off to the R.A.F. pilots. You are killing hundreds of Japs and your perfect co-ordination and patience in reading our crude signals is saving the lives of many thousands of defenceless civilians.'

Whilst these exploits revealed the magnificent work of aircrews, they illustrated at the same time the confidence and daring of the British-led irregular, for whom the pilots of Group squadrons felt most strongly that it was a case of 'Hats right off' to the guerrillas.

'From Letpangon we were attacked by two hundred Japs at 23.30 hours. We only killed fifteen of them, but we kept them there for you to attack next day when you put in two good strikes. They cleared out after dark and went on to Yindaikaein where you were able to attack them again,' said Captain Waller.

The combined attacks on the Japanese aircraft and guerrilla parties constituted a war of attrition on the enemy. They could never be sure of safety in any village they passed through, and roads, planked with thick scrub, were a perpetual nightmare. The guerrillas were masters in the art of ambush. With the air forces to supply and assist them they seemed to be everywhere, and to know the enemy's next move. This was evident from the casualties they inflicted against the Japanese.

It was after an attack by air forces on a large concentration of Japanese troops at Letpangon, that the Okpyat Guerrilla party, which had been pinning down the enemy until the aircraft arrived, went out in a most successful mopping-up task.

Captain Waller reported to the R.A.F., 'We only killed 15 of them but you killed 105 in three cracking good air strikes. You also saved the lives of almost three thousand occupants and evacuees in Okpyat who were completely cut off.'

Japanese Break-through from Pegu Yomas Fails
The desperate and last bid by the 28th Japanese Army to escape across the Sittang began on July 21st, when some 15,000 to 18,000 enemy troops, sick and demoralised, moved out of the jungle and scrub shelter of the Pegu Yomas.

The moment for which the squadrons and Allied ground forces had been awaiting had now come. The ground forces of 17 Indian Infantry Division, ranged in groups along the 100 miles stretch of roadway between Toungoo and Pegu, which formed part of the railway corridor, engaged the enemy, bursting over the road at several points simultaneously, and slaughtered them.

The squadrons of 221 Group were switched over to this battle area in support of 17 Division, and for almost nine days air assault was directed on the wretched Japanese as they made desperate attempts to reach the Sittang River.

From a captured enemy document it was revealed that the main breakthrough from the Pegu Yomas had been delayed by the enemy to allow the move of the Japanese 28th Army to co-ordinate. The greater part of the Mayazaki Group (Lt.-Gen. G.O.C. 54 Division) had planned to attempt to cross the Sittang between Nyaungbentha and Pyu. Coinciding with this move, Koba Group (Major-General Koba) had planned another major break out, and while the area of the move was not determined, it was anticipated that it would take place north of Toungoo in 19 Division area where troops were deploying along the Toungoo–Mawchi Road.

The enemy's plan was to form roadblocks at selected points and to pass through them assisted by 'Jitter Squads' to create diversions. All movements were to be made by night and the keynote of the break-through was to be 'speed' so that the maximum time would be available for the collection of boats and rafts from the Sittang river in order to complete the crossing before daylight. The enemy had planned, on reaching the Sittang to cross on a wide front using barges, rafts, logs, bamboo poles and even petrol tins to assist the buoyancy of escapees in the water.

It would be invidious to state that one squadron, more than another, inflicted the greatest punishment on the escaping enemy. All squadrons thrown into the 'Battle of the Break-through,' overcoming monsoon with low clouds and heavy rain for long periods, did what was expected of them with credit. The keenness of squadron ground personnel was equal to the occasion. They worked hard and ungrudgingly. All, indeed, in the air, as well as on the ground, felt that something substantial was being accomplished in this last show-down with the Japanese in Burma.

The July killing lasted until the 29th. The Thunderbolt squadrons, carrying three 500lb. bombs on each aircraft, played havoc among concentrations of moving Japanese troops. The Spitfires too, carrying one 500 lb. bomb on each aircraft, pursued the enemy relentlessly, strafing them as they ran for cover. As many as 62 sorties were flown on July 23rd by Nos. 152 and 155 Squadrons.

The extent of the full air effort by the R.A.F. squadrons in this battle cannot be adequately measured in the many squadron reports which told of the effectiveness and killings made during their strikes. The confusion and disruption caused among the Japanese forces, amounted to almost chaos. More convincing, perhaps, were the reports sent by 12th Army Divisional Commanders to H.Q. 221 Group, who were not slow to express their gratitude for the support given to their troops.

After almost nine days of intense fighting, the attempted break out by the Japanese from the Pegu Yomas ended in utter and complete failure. More than 10,000 men were killed, as against only three hundred odd casualties sustained by the Allied forces. Out of approximately 1,300 Japanese troops who succeeded in crossing the Sittang between Meikthalin and Wegyi, it was estimated that 500 of their number had been killed during air strikes by Spitfires and Thunderbolts. The whole Japanese plan for organised escape petered out in the closing days of July, and the air and ground attacks were then transferred once more to the Sittang Bend, where the other Japanese forces, to their credit, had held out bravely in their struggle to keep open the last doorway leading out of Burma. In the July battle, R.A.F. squadrons had flown a total of 3,045 sorties – 92 per cent. of which were offensive strikes in support of ground troops, while a total weight of 1,490,000 lb. of bombs had been dropped.

As the last few hundreds of exhausted Japanese were making their escape to Moulmein with bitter recollections of the ordeal they had passed through, Lieutenant-General Sir Montague Stopford, G.O.C. 12th Army, when recalling the severity of the weather, its flooding, rains and cloud, showed his appreciation of the RA.F. in these words:

> Grateful if you would accept and pass on to all ranks under your command my most grateful thanks for the admirable support given during break-out battle and my congratulations on splendid results achieved. Flying conditions must have been most difficult but on all sides I hear nothing but praise of the keenness and determination of pilots to get through. You have all played a great part in the Twelfth Army's first big operation.

Over and above the R.A.F. contribution, our victory was won by our superiority over the Japanese in training, fighting ability and weapons; the accurate intelligence which was obtained before the battle began; the fine work of the guerrillas, and above all the high morale and fighting efficiency of the troops.

Appendix IV

Extract from Air Chief Marshal Park's Despatch on Air Operations in South-East Asia, 3 May 1945 to 12 September 1945: Operations Birdcage and Mastiff: The Liberation of Allied Prisoners of War and Internees

The relief and liberation of almost 100,000 Allied prisoners-of-war and internees confined in Japanese prison camps throughout the vast territories of South East Asia, is an episode in the Far Eastern War which relied almost entirely upon Air Power for its success in the initial but vital stages of its operation.

It would be inaccurate to record that the Air Forces alone were responsible for the ultimate rescue and liberation of these thousands of prisoners, but the Air Forces of this Command carried out vital tasks as follows:

(a) Spread the news of Japanese surrender in millions of leaflets dropped over the principal towns and known sites of Japanese prison camps scattered throughout South East Asia.
(b) Warned Allied prisoners-of-war and internees of their impending liberation.
(c) Dropped medical supplies, medical teams, administrative personnel and W/T operators to make first contact with prisoners and to signal back vital information regarding numbers imprisoned and supplies required.
(d) Air dropped, or air landed, quantities of food, clothing and other necessities to relieve the privations suffered at prison camps.
(e) Evacuated by air hundreds of prisoners from Malaya, Siam, French Indo-China, Sumatra and Java, including cases of very serious illness.

In a message to all formations of Air Command which took part in the inauguration of this task on August 28th, 1945, the operation was described as 'the greatest mercy mission of the war'.

It was a mission of paramount importance to thousands of families in Britain, the Dominions and, indeed, in Holland, who eagerly awaited information about relatives interned and captured during the Japanese conquest of Malaya in 1942.

In Singapore alone, about 35,000 prisoners were held in the various Japanese prison camps throughout Singapore Island the most notorious of which was the Changi Gaol. The inmates of these camps had been subjected to coarse indignities and even torture.

The feeling in Britain found expression in a message from the British Foreign Secretary to the Supreme Allied Commander, South East Asia, in which he drew Admiral Mountbatten's attention to the numerous enquiries which the Government had received since the publication of atrocity stories from Singapore and elsewhere, and saying that there was grave concern in respect of Sumatra, since deaths actually reported by the Japanese through the International Red Cross were much higher in proportion to numbers anywhere else in the Far East.

It can be seen, therefore, how well suited was Air Power to perform this vitally important task involving great distances across great tracts of land – a task also in which speed was essential for its success.

Operation 'Birdcage' launched.
As soon as the Japanese surrender had been universally accepted and confirmed, action was taken to issue instructions contained in specially prepared leaflets to:-

(a) Japanese Prison Guards.
(b) Allied Prisoners-of-war.
(c) Local Japanese forces.
(d) The local native population.

The operation to implement this action was allotted the code name of *Birdcage* and was launched by the Air Forces of Air Command on August 28th, operating from bases in Ceylon, Cocos Islands, Bengal and Burma.

Thereafter, Operation *Mastiff*, was planned to ensure that medical aid, comforts, food, clothing, R.A.P.W.I. Control Staffs where necessary, and any other essential preliminary needs were introduced into the camps as early as possible.

Operation *Birdcage* was completed by August 31st. In the space of four days, leaflets had been dropped over 236 localities and 90 prisoner-of-war camps throughout Burma, Siam, French Indo-China, Malaya and Sumatra. Where sorties were at first rendered abortive by weather and by difficulty in locating targets or by mechanical trouble, they were persisted with on the following days. Very few priority targets remained uncovered. One group of towns in the hinterland of Malaya was successfully covered only at the third attempt.

In addition to Liberator sorties flown from bases in Ceylon, Cocos Islands and Bengal, Thunderbolts operating from Burma dropped one million leaflets on thirteen localities in Southern Burma extending as far south as the Kra

Isthmus. No target was left uncovered. One Thunderbolt was lost during these operations – the aircraft crashing in flames at Kraburi.

I think it is worthy of note that Operation *Birdcage* was carried out in very indifferent conditions. Even more important still was the fact that an all round trip of many of the sorties was equivalent to a trans-Atlantic flight. Nevertheless, 75 per cent. of the crews reached their targets, which included towns and camps as far east as Hanoi, Tourane and Saigon.

Success of Leaflet Dropping.
The news of Japanese surrender contained in the millions of leaflets dropped met with great enthusiasm throughout the scattered territories of South East Asia. They were picked up on the streets of towns and read eagerly by the civilian population. The messages also dropped to the Allied prisoners-of-war stated, 'We want to get you back home quickly, safe and sound'.

Many of the prisoners had been Japanese forced labour for the building of the notorious Bangkok-Moulmein railway – a slave task which will take its place among the list of incredible efforts carried out by captive men.

August, 1945, saw the greatest effort in leaflet dropping attempted by aircraft of the Command.

Prior to the surrender, and immediately after, some 33,000,000 leaflets were dropped over the enemy-occupied territories in South East Asia. This form of psychological warfare had been stepped up very considerably after the defeat of the Japanese in Burma, and in July the total dropped by aircraft of the Command reached 22,000,000.

One particular form of leaflet, dropped over the trapped Japanese forces in the Pegu Yomas of Southern Burma during July, not only called upon the enemy to surrender after telling them of the hopeless position of their homeland, but, on the reverse side offered them a safe conduct through the Allied lines with the added assurance that they would be given food, medical attention and honourable treatment.

Launching of Operation 'Mastiff'.
The saturating of towns and prison camps with leaflets announcing the Japanese surrender was, in itself, a laudable effort, but the main task which awaited the Air Forces was unquestionably that of Operation *Mastiff* in bringing practical relief and comfort to those who needed them most.

Hundreds of these prisoners were emaciated, gaunt and pitiful beings – some, indeed, were too weak to stand upon their legs. The majority of prisoners were deficient of proper clothing. There were instances too, where some were completely naked.

The need of medical supplies was perhaps the greatest, for the Japanese had shown little ability or willingness to appreciate the needs of prisoners-of-war in many cases. The immediate requirements in drugs, therefore, could only be taken to sufferers by air, and, as a large percentage of prisoners and internees, particularly in Singapore, were affected by malaria, it was estimated that 1.250,000 tablets of Atabrine, or substitute, were essential for delivery each week.

The *Mastiff* operation in the early stages was carried out by ten Liberator squadrons (including one R.A.A.F. squadron) and one Dakota squadron. Three Liberator squadrons operated from bases in Bengal – Jessore, Salbani and Digri – covering targets chiefly in Siam and French Indo-China. From bases in Ceylon another three Liberator squadrons operated over Malaya and Sumatra, while areas in Malaya and Java were supplied by three Liberator squadrons based in the Cocos Islands, though these were chiefly employed on targets in Sumatra.

The Dakota squadron operated from Rangoon over Siam and the Tenasserim Coastal Area of Southern Burma. The tasks undertaken by this Dakota squadron must not be confused with the all-out effort made by five Dakota squadrons of No. 232 Group, R.A.F., based on Rangoon, which were employed on the air-lift to Bangkok, where the Don Muang Airfield was quickly in use. The operations of these Dakota squadrons in the air landing of supplies and in the evacuation of prisoners-of-war was one of the outstanding features of the air operations associated with *Mastiff*.

From 1st to 5th September, approximately 200 Dakota sorties were flown from Rangoon, and some 400 tons of stores were dropped or landed. The same aircraft carried back 4,000 prisoners-of-war and internees. On the following week the Dakotas carried out a further 360 sorties and dropped or landed 600 tons of stores. On their return trips they carried back some 3,700 prisoners-of-war. It as a tribute to the enthusiasm shown by the Dakota aircrews at this time that 12th Army, by September 10th, was able to report that approximately 9,000 prisoners-of-war had been carried back to Rangoon from Bangkok. Early in the month, practically all the U.S. prisoners-of-war had been evacuated from the Bangkok area, the figure being approximately 162. This evacuation was carried out chiefly by U.S. airlift, which was also responsible for bringing out a number of British and Allied sick.

Use of Thunderbolts and R.A.A.F. Liberators.
Though not actually engaged upon Operation 'Mastiff', a number of Thunderbolt aircraft flew from their bases in Burma and assisted in the problem of locating camps and determining their circumstances. Many of these Thunderbolt sorties were rendered abortive by weather, but other sorties resulted in the bringing back of valuable information. It was noted, for example, that several of the prison camps on the Burma-Siam railway, in the area stretching N.W. from Kanchanaburi, were deserted and empty, while prisoners-of-war in other scattered camps greeted the appearance of the Thunderbolts with understandable enthusiasm expressed by frantic cheering and waving.

Appendix V

Reproduction of pages from Angus Findon's Pilot's Logbook

ROYAL CANADIAN
AIR FORCE

PILOT'S FLYING
LOG BOOK

Name FINDON

(All images courtesy of the John Gadd Collection)

YEAR 1943		AIRCRAFT		PILOT, OR 1ST PILOT	2ND PILOT, PUPIL OR PASSENGER	DUTY (INCLUDING RESULTS AND REMARKS)
MONTH	DATE	Type	No.			TOTALS BROUGHT FORWARD
					No. 9 E. F. T. S.	
Jan	17	T. Moth	T.5467	Sgt. Berryman	Self	1.2.3.
"	18	T. Moth	N.6621	Sgt. Paine	Self	1.2.4.5.6.
"	18	T. Moth	N.6621	Sgt. Paine	Self	2.5.6.7.8.9.
"	20	T. Moth	A.4921	Sgt. Parker	Self	1.5.6.7.8.14. 4 Spins
"	21	T. Moth	T.7751	P/O Knowler	Self	1.10.11.12.
"	21	T. Moth	T.7751	P/O Knowler	Self	5.12.13 (1.)
"	26	T. Moth	N.6612	Sgt. Paine	Self	12.13 (1)
"	26	T. Moth	N.6612	Sgt. Paine	Self	12.13. (1.2.)
"	27	T. Moth	N.6612	Sgt. Paine	Self	10.11.12.13. (1.)

GRAND TOTAL [Cols. (1) to (10)]
6 Hrs 50 Mins.

TOTALS CARRIED FORWARD

Appendix V 129

SINGLE-ENGINE AIRCRAFT				MULTI-ENGINE AIRCRAFT						PASS-ENGER	INSTR/CLOUD FLYING [incl. in cols. (1) to (10)]		LINK TRAINER
DAY		NIGHT		DAY			NIGHT						
DUAL	PILOT	DUAL	PILOT	DUAL	1ST PILOT	2ND PILOT	DUAL	1ST PILOT	2ND PILOT		DUAL	PILOT	
(1)	(2)	(3)	(4)	(5)	(6)	(7)	(8)	(9)	(10)	(11)	(12)	(13)	(14)
				A N S T Y									
·50													
·35													
·55													
·50													
·60													
·35													
·40													
·50													
·35													
6·50													
(1)	(2)	(3)	(4)	(5)	(6)	(7)	(8)	(9)	(10)	(11)	(12)	(13)	(14)

Year 1943 Month	Date	Aircraft Type	No.	Pilot, or 1st Pilot	2nd Pilot, Pupil or Passenger	Duty (Including Results and Remarks)
		—	—	—	—	Totals Brought Forward
Jan.	27	T. Moth.	N6612	Sgt. Paine.	Self.	12. 13. (1.)
"	28	T. Moth.	T.7751	F/O Laverton.	Self.	7 Hour Test.
Feb	2	T. Moth.	N.6865	Sgt. Paine.	Self.	7. 8. 13. (1) 14 6 Spins
"	3	T. Moth.	N.6865	Sgt. Paine.	Self.	12. 13. (1)
"	4	T. Moth.	T.6101	Sgt. Paine.	Self.	12. 13. (1) 14 4 Spins.
"	7	T. Moth.	T.6101	Sgt. Paine.	Self.	12. 13. (1)
"	7	T. Moth.	N.7751	F/O. Laverton.	Self.	12 Hour Test.
						Course Total.

Grand Total [Cols. (1) to (10)] 12 Hrs. 30 Mins.   Totals Carried Forward

Soon after you left I renewed my search for a booklet which was such a joy to receive it is still a bit of a thrill to touch. I'll give it to you next time we meet rather than risk its loss in the post. This little Air Ministry publication says boldly on its cover - "You Are Going To Be A Pilot". We were given this at a great assembly in a Manchester cinema when the result of our grading course at Ansty was announced. We were told that our number and name would be called out, together with the role for which we had been selected. Those not selected for pilot training were to answer, 'Sir, I understand', the rest simply answered, 'Sir'.

Having failed to solo at Ansty I braced myself for disappointment. Then the voice said, '1806476 L.A.C. Findon, Pilot.'

My immense happiness was only spoilt to a degree by the awful disappointment some of the other chaps had to face. Some of course did not mind at all, they had no desire to become "Drivers, airframe."

YEAR 1943	AIRCRAFT		PILOT, OR 1ST PILOT	2ND PILOT, PUPIL OR PASSENGER	DUTY (INCLUDING RESULTS AND REMARKS)
MONTH DATE	Type	No.			TOTALS BROUGHT FORWARD
				No. 31	E. F. T. S.
					COURSE
May 30	CORNELL	10646	F/O. Gibson.	SELF	1.A. FAMILIARIZATION-GROUND
					1.B. FAMILIARIZATION - AIR.
					1.C. TARMAC CHECK.
					2. THE FLYING CONTROLS
					3. TAXYING.
					4. STRAIGHT & LEVEL FLIGHT
					5. CLIMBING, DESCENDING, Gliding
May 31	CORNELL	10668	F/O. Gibson.	SELF.	2. THE FLYING CONTROLS.
					3. TAXYING.
					4. STRAIGHT & LEVEL FLIGHT
					5. CLIMBING, DESCENDING, GLIDING
					5.A. STALLING.
					6. TURNING.
					10A. SPINNING FROM CLIMBING TURN
					10B. SPINNING FROM GLIDING TURN
					10.C. SPINNING FROM STEEP TURN
					2A. 2L
			GRAND TOTAL [Cols. (1) to (10)] .... Hrs .... Mins.		TOTALS CARRIED FORWARD

Appendix V   133

SINGLE-ENGINE AIRCRAFT				MULTI-ENGINE AIRCRAFT								PASS-ENGER	INSTR/CLOUD FLYING [Incl. in cols. (1) to (10)]		LINK TRAINER
DAY		NIGHT		DAY			NIGHT						
DUAL	PILOT	DUAL	PILOT	DUAL	1ST PILOT	2ND PILOT	DUAL	1ST PILOT	2ND PILOT		DUAL	PILOT	
(1)	(2)	(3)	(4)	(5)	(6)	(7)	(8)	(9)	(10)	(11)	(12)	(13)	(14)

De WINTON.

No. 82.

FAIRCHILD CORNELL TRAINERS

·45·

·50

·95

YEAR 1943		AIRCRAFT		PILOT, OR 1ST PILOT	2ND PILOT, PUPIL OR PASSENGER	DUTY (INCLUDING RESULTS AND REMARKS)
MONTH	DATE	Type	No.			TOTALS BROUGHT FORWARD
June	1	Cornell	15024	F/O. Gibson	Self	3. Taxiing.
						4. Straight & Level Flight
						5. Climbing. Descending. Gliding
						6A. Climbing Turns.
						6B. Descending Turns.
						6C. Gliding Turns.
						5A. Stalling.
						7. Take Off.
						8. Gliding. Approach & Landing
						10A. Spin From Climbing Turn.
						10B. Spin From Gliding Turn.
						10C. Spin From Steep Turn.
						2R. 2L.
June	3	Cornell	15024	F/O. Gibson	Self	6A. Climbing Turns.
						6B. Descending Turns.
						6C. Gliding Turns.
						7. Take Off.
						8. Approach & Landing
June	4	Cornell	10669	F/O. Gibson	Self	6A. Climbing Turns.
						6B. Descending Turns.
						6C. Gliding Turns.

GRAND TOTAL [Cols. (1) to (10)]
_____ Hrs. _____ Mins.   TOTALS CARRIED FORWARD

Appendix V 135

SINGLE-ENGINE AIRCRAFT				MULTI-ENGINE AIRCRAFT						PASS-ENGER	INSTR/CLOUD FLYING [Incl. in cols. (1) to (10)]		LINK TRAINER
DAY		NIGHT		DAY			NIGHT						
DUAL	PILOT	DUAL	PILOT	DUAL	1ST PILOT	2ND PILOT	DUAL	1ST PILOT	2ND PILOT		DUAL	PILOT	
(1)	(2)	(3)	(4)	(5)	(6)	(7)	(8)	(9)	(10)	(11)	(12)	(13)	(14)
·95													
1·05													
1·00													
3·40													
(1)	(2)	(3)	(4)	(5)	(6)	(7)	(8)	(9)	(10)	(11)	(12)	(13)	(14)

YEAR 1943		AIRCRAFT		PILOT, OR 1ST PILOT	2ND PILOT, PUPIL OR PASSENGER	DUTY (INCLUDING RESULTS AND REMARKS)
MONTH	DATE	Type	No.			TOTALS BROUGHT FORWARD
June	6	Cornell	15013	Sgt. England	Self	6a. Climbing Turns. 6b. Descending Turns 6c. Gliding Turns. 7. Take Off. 8. Gliding Approach & Landing 9. Engine Assisted Approach
June	7	Cornell	10675	Sgt. England	Self	7. Take Off 8. Gliding Approach & Landing 9. Engine Assisted Approach
June	10	Cornell	15023	Sgt. England	Self	6. Turning. 7. Take Off. 8. Gliding Approach & Landing 9. Engine Assisted Approach
June	10	Cornell	10657	F/O. Gibson	Self	10a. Spinning from Straight Glide (12 IR) Solo Test.
						WEEKLY TOTAL COURSE TOTAL

GRAND TOTAL [Cols. (1) to (10)]
09 Hrs. 00 Mins.   TOTALS CARRIED FORWARD

Appendix V   137

SINGLE-ENGINE AIRCRAFT				MULTI-ENGINE AIRCRAFT							PASS-ENGER	INSTR/CLOUD FLYING [incl. in cols. (1) to (10)]		LINK TRAINER
DAY		NIGHT		DAY			NIGHT							
DUAL	PILOT	DUAL	PILOT	DUAL	1ST PILOT	2ND PILOT	DUAL	1ST PILOT	2ND PILOT		DUAL	PILOT	
(1)	(2)	(3)	(4)	(5)	(6)	(7)	(8)	(9)	(10)	(11)	(12)	(13)	(14)
5·40													
1·00													
·45													
·45													
·50													
3·20													
09·00													

| (1) | (2) | (3) | (4) | (5) | (6) | (7) | (8) | (9) | (10) | (11) | (12) | (13) | (14) |

Year 1943		Aircraft		Pilot, or 1st Pilot	2nd Pilot, Pupil or Passenger	Duty (Including Results and Remarks)
Month	Date	Type	No.			Totals Brought Forward
June	12	Cornell	16643	Self	Solo.	First Solo.
June	12	Cornell	16643	Sgt England	Self	6. Turning. 7. Take Off. 8. Gliding Approach & Landing
June	13	Cornell	15023	Sgt England	Self	6. Turning. 7. Take Off. 8. Gliding Approach & Landing.
June	13	Cornell	15023	Self	Solo.	7. Take Off. 8. Gliding Approach & Landing 9. Engine Assisted Approach.
June	14	D. Link	334	Sgt Spencer	Self	1-2-3 System of Instrument Flying. 2. Straight Course
June	15	D. Link	546	Sgt Spencer	Self	3. Straight & Level Flight
June	15	Cornell	15006	Sgt England	Self	6. Turning 7. Take Off. 9. Engine Assisted Approach

GRAND TOTAL [Cols. (1) to (10)] 11:00 Hrs. 25 Mins.   Totals Carried Forward

SINGLE-ENGINE AIRCRAFT				MULTI-ENGINE AIRCRAFT							PASS-ENGER	INSTR/CLOUD FLYING [incl. in cols. (1) to (10)]		LINK TRAINER
DAY		NIGHT		DAY			NIGHT					
DUAL	PILOT	DUAL	PILOT	DUAL	1ST PILOT	2ND PILOT	DUAL	1ST PILOT	2ND PILOT		DUAL	PILOT	
(1)	(2)	(3)	(4)	(5)	(6)	(7)	(8)	(9)	(10)	(11)	(12)	(13)	(14)
09·00													
	20												
35													
20													
	45												
													·15
													·45
													·60
25													
10·20	1·05												
(1)	(2)	(3)	(4)	(5)	(6)	(7)	(8)	(9)	(10)	(11)	(12)	(13)	(14)

YEAR 1943		AIRCRAFT		PILOT, OR 1ST PILOT	2ND PILOT, PUPIL OR PASSENGER	DUTY (INCLUDING RESULTS AND REMARKS)
MONTH	DATE	Type	No.			
						TOTALS BROUGHT FORWARD
						No. 1 F.I.S
DEC.	15	HARVARD I	2684	F/L PERODEAU	SELF	FAMILIARIZATION.
DEC.	15	HARVARD I	2684	SELF	SOLO	5. 7. 8. 9.
						10a. SPIN FROM A STRAIGHT GLIDE
						17. FORCED LANDING
						22. AEROBATICS
DEC.	16	CORNELL	675	F/L PERODEAU	SELF	FAMILIARIZATION.
DEC.	16	CORNELL	675	SELF	SOLO	9, 11, 12, 13, 14, 21, 22.
DEC.	17	CORNELL	749	F/L PERODEAU	SELF	10. 5. 12. 13. 21. 22. 23.
DEC.	17	CORNELL	749	SELF	P/O HARVIE	5. 12. 13. 21. 22.
DEC.	17	CORNELL	749	P/O HARVIE	SELF	REFRESHER.
DEC.	18	CORNELL	675	F/L PERODEAU	SELF	4. 10. 21. 22.
DEC.	18	CORNELL	761	SELF	P/O PICHER	4. 13. 21.
DEC.	18	CORNELL	761	P/O PICHER	SELF	
						WEEK TOTAL.
						No. 1 F.I.S TOTAL.
						GRAND TOTAL.
DEC.	21	CORNELL	749	F/L PERODEAU	SELF	4. 9. 14.
DEC.	20	CORNELL	749	F/L PERODEAU	SELF	INSTRUMENTS.
DEC.	22	CORNELL	749	P/O PICHER	SELF	
DEC.	22	CORNELL	749	SELF	P/O PICHER	13. 14. 22.

O.C. "B" FLIGHT

GRAND TOTAL [Cols. (1) to (10)] 264 Hrs. 60 Mins.   TOTALS CARRIED FORWARD

Appendix V 141

SINGLE-ENGINE AIRCRAFT				MULTI-ENGINE AIRCRAFT						PASS-ENGER	INSTR/CLOUD FLYING [incl. in cols. (1) to (10)]		LINK TRAINER
DAY		NIGHT		DAY			NIGHT				DUAL	PILOT	
DUAL	PILOT	DUAL	PILOT	DUAL	1ST PILOT	2ND PILOT	DUAL	1ST PILOT	2ND PILOT			
(1)	(2)	(3)	(4)	(5)	(6)	(7)	(8)	(9)	(10)	(11)	(12)	(13)	(14)
138.35	89.45	13.30	11.45							13.50	41.00	00.10	37.00
				T R E N T O N.			O N T.						
1.00													
	.40												
.50													
	1.00												
1.40													
.50	.50												
1.00													
	.30										.30		
5.10	2.10									1.20			
5.20	2.10									1.20			
147.15	91.55	13.30	11.45							15.10	41.00	00.10	37.00
1.00													
1.00											1.00		
										.45			
	.45												
145.25	93.30	13.30	11.45							15.55	42.00	00.10	37.00
(1)	(2)	(3)	(4)	(5)	(6)	(7)	(8)	(9)	(10)	(11)	(12)	(13)	(14)

142 *Thunderbolts over Burma*

YEAR 1943-4		AIRCRAFT		PILOT, OR 1ST PILOT	2ND PILOT, PUPIL OR PASSENGER	DUTY (INCLUDING RESULTS AND REMARKS)
MONTH	DATE	Type	No.			
—	—	—	—	—	—	TOTALS BROUGHT FORWARD
DEC.	22	HARVARD II	2560	P/O PENDLEBURY	SELF	28. FORMATION
						WEEK TOTAL
				O.C. "B" FLIGHT		COURSE TOTAL
						GRAND TOTAL
DEC.	29	CORNELL	749	P/O PICHER	SELF	
DEC.	29	CORNELL	749	SELF	P/O PICHER	10. 13. 21. 22. 25.
DEC.	29	CORNELL	749	F/L PERODEAU	SELF	4
DEC.	29	CORNELL	749	F/L PERODEAU	SELF	9. 10. 19.
DEC.	31	HARVARD	2684	F/L PERODEAU	SELF	INSTRUMENTS
DEC.	31	CORNELL	761	F/L PERODEAU	SELF	9. 10. 13. 14.
DEC.	31	CORNELL	675	SELF	P/O SCOTT	4. 9. 10. 13. 14. 19. 21. 22. 25.
JAN.	2	HARVARD	FE560	S/P EASEY	SELF	
JAN.	2	HARVARD	FE560	SELF	S/P EASEY	6. 9. 10. 13. 14. 19. 21. 22.
JAN.	2	HARVARD	BW.197	S/P EASEY	SELF	
JAN.	2	HARVARD	BW.197	SELF	S/P EASEY	9. 10. 13. 14. 19. 21. 22.
				O.C. "B" FLIGHT		WEEK TOTAL
						COURSE TOTAL
						GRAND TOTAL
JAN.	3	CORNELL	EH.749	F/L PERODEAU	SELF	9. 10. 13. 14. 19. 21. 22. 25.
JAN.	3	CORNELL	EH.749	F/O EAKINS	SELF	PATTER TEST
JAN.	3	HARVARD I	FE560	SELF	S/P EASEY	14. 25. 13.
JAN.	4	HARVARD II	BW.197	F/L PERODEAU	SELF	20. 21. 22. 25.

GRAND TOTAL [Cols. (1) to (10)]
296 Hrs. 40 Mins.   TOTALS CARRIED FORWARD

Appendix V   143

SINGLE-ENGINE AIRCRAFT				MULTI-ENGINE AIRCRAFT						PASS-ENGER	INSTR/CLOUD FLYING [Incl. in cols. (1) to (10)]		LINK TRAINER
DAY		NIGHT		DAY			NIGHT						
DUAL	PILOT	DUAL	PILOT	DUAL	1ST PILOT	2ND PILOT	DUAL	1ST PILOT	2ND PILOT		DUAL	PILOT	
(1)	(2)	(3)	(4)	(5)	(6)	(7)	(8)	(9)	(10)	(11)	(12)	(13)	(14)
145·25	93·30	13·30	11·45							15·55	42·00	00·10	37·00
1·10													
3·10	·45									·45	1·00		EJ
7·40	3·45									2·05	1·00		
146·35	93·30	13·30	11·45							18·45	42·00	00·10	37·00
	·35									·35			
·30													
1·15													
1·15											1·15		
1·00													
	1·45												
	·40									·40			
										·45			
	·45									2·00	1·15		
4·00	3·45									4·05	2·15		MJ
11·40	7·30									17·55	43·15	00·10	37·00
150·35	97·15	13·30											
1·45													
·50													
	1·20												
1·45													
154·55	98·35	13·30	11·45							17·55	43·15	00·10	37·00
(1)	(2)	(3)	(4)	(5)	(6)	(7)	(8)	(9)	(10)	(11)	(12)	(13)	(14)

YEAR 1943		AIRCRAFT		PILOT, OR 1ST PILOT	2ND PILOT, PUPIL OR PASSENGER	DUTY (INCLUDING RESULTS AND REMARKS)
MONTH	DATE	Type	No.			TOTALS BROUGHT FORWARD
						73. O.T.U. FAYID
Nov.	22	HARVARD II	EZ.398	F/O CARROL	SELF	Ex. 1, 3.
Nov.	24	HARVARD II	EZ.249	F/O CARROL	SELF	Ex. 1, 2.
Nov.	24	HARVARD II	EZ.249	SELF	SOLO	Ex. 3.
Nov.	24	HARVARD II	EZ.249	SELF	SOLO	Ex. 5.
Nov.	27	HARVARD II	EZ.249	F/O LAPOINTE	SELF	Ex. 1. 2. 3. 4. 6.
Nov.	27	HARVARD II	EZ.352	P/O COLYER	SELF	FLIGHT COMMANDER'S CHECK
Nov.	29	HARVARD II	EZ.926	SELF	—	AEROBATICS
Nov.	29	THUNDERBOLT	KJ.137	SELF	—	FIRST SOLO.
Nov.	29	HARVARD II	EZ.344	SELF	P/O LAPOINTE	TO SATELITE OR RETURN.
		SUMMARY FOR NOVEMBER 1944		HARVARD II	MONTH TOTAL	
		UNIT. 73. O.T.U. DATE 30/11/44		THUNDERBOLT	COURSE TOTAL	
		SIGNATURE A. Findon				
Dec.	1	THUNDERBOLT	H.D.139	SELF	—	STEEP TURNS. CIRCUITS.
Dec.	1	THUNDERBOLT	KJ.143	SELF	—	FORCED LANDINGS. LOW FLYING.
Dec.	4	THUNDERBOLT	H.D.143	SELF	—	D/F HOMINGS. FORCED LANDINGS.
Dec.	6	THUNDERBOLT	FL.824	SELF	—	CROSS COUNTRY.
Dec.	8	THUNDERBOLT	FL.824	SELF	—	FORMATION.
		UNIT: 73 O.T.U.		SUMMARY FOR		
		DATE 8/12/44		1 SQUADRON	AIRCRAFT TYPES	HARVARD II THUNDERBOLT
		SIGNATURE A. Findon				

GRAND TOTAL [Cols. (1) to (10)]
400 Hrs. 10 Mins.   TOTALS CARRIED FORWARD

Appendix V   145

Single-Engine Aircraft				Multi-Engine Aircraft						PASS-ENGER	INSTR/CLOUD FLYING [Incl. in cols. (1) to (10)]		LINK TRAINER
DAY		NIGHT		DAY			NIGHT							
DUAL	PILOT	DUAL	PILOT	DUAL	1ST PILOT	2ND PILOT	DUAL	1ST PILOT	2ND PILOT		DUAL	PILOT	
(1)	(2)	(3)	(4)	(5)	(6)	(7)	(8)	(9)	(10)	(11)	(12)	(13)	(14)
188.20	152.15	21.10	18.00	1.10						41.55	53.40	2.10	59.45
EGYPT													
2.15													
1.30													
	.30												
	.50												
1.45													
1.20													
	1.00												
	2.00												
	.30												
6.50	4.50												
6.50	4.50				E.Ricardo F/O							
					O.C. 'C' Flt.						O.C. FLYING		
	2.00												
	1.10												
	1.30												.30	
	1.35												.20	
	1.20												
6.50	2.50								E.Ricardo F/O.C.		'C' Flt.		
	9.35												
195.10	164.40	21.10	18.00	1.10						41.55	53.40	5.00	59.45
(1)	(2)	(3)	(4)	(5)	(6)	(7)	(8)	(9)	(10)	(11)	(12)	(13)	(14)

Year 1944-5		Aircraft		Pilot, or 1st Pilot	2nd Pilot, Pupil or Passenger	Duty (Including Results and Remarks)
Month	Date	Type	No.			Totals Brought Forward
Dec	12	Thunderbolt	FL802	Self	—	Oxygen Climb. Battle Formation.
Dec	12	Thunderbolt	J.K.143	Self	—	Oxygen Climb. 42,000
Dec	14	Thunderbolt	FL829	Self	—	Oxygen Climb & Aerobatics
Dec	14	Thunderbolt	FL829	Self	—	Battle Formation.
Dec	16	Thunderbolt	K.J.185	Self	—	Battle Formation. Section Attacks
Dec	16	Thunderbolt	K.J.185	Self	—	Individual Attacks.
Dec	19	Thunderbolt	H.D.138	Self	—	Battle Formation. Section Attacks
Dec	21	Thunderbolt	J.K.143	Self	—	Individual Attacks.
Dec	28	Thunderbolt	FL824	Self	—	Individual Opp. Attacks
Dec	28	Thunderbolt	FL829	Self	—	Aerobatics.
Dec	28	Thunderbolt	FL829	Self	—	Aerobatics.
Dec	30	Thunderbolt	K.J.147	Self	—	Battle Formation.
		Unit:		73 O.T.U. Fayid.	Summary for 2 Sqdn.	A/C Type: Thunderbolt
		Date:		30 Dec. 1943		
		Signature:		A. Lindon		
Jan	1	Thunderbolt	H.D.125	Self	—	Ciné 1.
Jan	1	Thunderbolt	K.J.142	Self	—	Ciné 1.2.2.
Jan	2	Harvard	Z	F/O Brooks		
Jan	3	Thunderbolt	K.J.142	Self	—	Bombing. Ciné 2.2.3.
Jan	3	Harvard	Z	W/O. Simmons		A to G
Jan	3	Thunderbolt		Self	—	Bombing. Ciné 2.2.3.
Jan	4	Harvard	W	F/O Mansfield	Self	Ciné 4. 5.

GRAND TOTAL [Cols. (1) to (10)]
427 Hrs. 30 Mins.   Totals Carried Forward

Appendix V 147

SINGLE-ENGINE AIRCRAFT				MULTI-ENGINE AIRCRAFT						PASS-ENGER	INSTR/CLOUD FLYING (Incl. in cols. (1) to (10))		LINK TRAINER
DAY		NIGHT		DAY			NIGHT						
DUAL	PILOT	DUAL	PILOT	DUAL	1ST PILOT	2ND PILOT	DUAL	1ST PILOT	2ND PILOT		DUAL	PILOT	
(1)	(2)	(3)	(4)	(5)	(6)	(7)	(8)	(9)	(10)	(11)	(12)	(13)	(14)
195.10	164.40	21.10	18.00	1.10						41.55	53.40	5.00	59.45
	1.45												
	1.20												
	2.00												
	1.40												
	1.50			YIMKIN = MAYBE									
	1.15			IN ARABIC									
	2.00												
	2.00												
	1.50												
	1.50												
	1.30												
	2.00												
	21.40												
	1.10												
	1.15												
.45													
	2.00												
1.00													
	1.30												
.40													
197.35	191.35	21.10	18.00	1.10						41.55	53.40	5.00	59.45
(1)	(2)	(3)	(4)	(5)	(6)	(7)	(8)	(9)	(10)	(11)	(12)	(13)	(14)

Year 1945		Aircraft		Pilot, or 1st Pilot	2nd Pilot, Pupil or Passenger	Duty (Including Results and Remarks)
Month	Date	Type	No.			
						Totals Brought Forward
Jan.	5.	Thunderbolt	FL.829	Self.	—	Bombing. Cine 4 a.a.k
Jan.	5.	Thunderbolt	KJ.185	Self.	—	A to G.
Jan.	8.	Thunderbolt	KJ.353	Self.	—	A. to G.
Jan.	8.	Thunderbolt	FL.154	Self.	—	A. to G.
Jan.	9.	Thunderbolt	KJ.159	Self.	—	Bombing and Cine's
Jan.	9.	Thunderbolt	KJ.353	Self.	—	A. to G.
Jan.	12.	Harvard	FX.839	W/O Weatherstone	Self	A to H.
Jan.	12.	Thunderbolt	KJ.159	Self.	Solo	Bombing and Cine's.
Jan.	12.	Thunderbolt	FL.154	Self.	—	Air to Air.
Jan.	15.	Thunderbolt	KJ.185	Self.	—	Air to Air.
Jan.	15.	Harvard	W	W/O Simmons.	Self.	Air to Air.
Jan.	17.	Thunderbolt	KJ.353	Self.	—	Air to Air.
Jan.	18.	Thunderbolt	FL.154	Self.	—	Bombing and Cine's
				Summary For:	Air Firing Squadron.	Thunderbolt.
		J.Brooks S/L		Unit:	73. O.T.U.	Harvard.
		O.C. 'S' Flight.		Date:	18:1:45.	
				Signature:	A. Findon.	
				Summary For:	73. O.T.U.	
				Unit:	73. O.T.U.	Thunderbolt.
				Date:	18:1:45.	Harvard.
				Signature:	A. Findon.	
Feb.	11.	Sunderland	S/L X.	Self		Nile - Basra - Karachi

GRAND TOTAL [Cols. (1) to (10)]
445 Hrs. 50 Mins.
Totals Carried Forward

SINGLE-ENGINE AIRCRAFT				MULTI-ENGINE AIRCRAFT						PASS-ENGER	INSTR/CLOUD FLYING [incl. in cols. (1) to (10)]		LINK TRAINER
DAY		NIGHT		DAY			NIGHT						
DUAL	PILOT	DUAL	PILOT	DUAL	1ST PILOT	2ND PILOT	DUAL	1ST PILOT	2ND PILOT		DUAL	PILOT	
(1)	(2)	(3)	(4)	(5)	(6)	(7)	(8)	(9)	(10)	(11)	(12)	(13)	(14)
197.35	191.35	21·10	18·00	1·10						41·55	53·40	5·00	59·45
	1·45												

FLYING ASSESSMENT FOR 32 COURSE 73. O.T.U.

TYPE OF AIRCRAFT	COURSE TOTALS				GRAND TOTALS			
	DUAL		SOLO		DUAL		SOLO	
	Day	N/F	Day	N/F	Day	N/F	Day	N/F
1. HARVARD			2·50		90·00	13·15	59·35	13·00
2. THUNDERBOLT			51·05				51·05	
3.								

ASSESSMENT.
: Fighter Tactics. Proficient
: Formation Flying Proficient

Exceptional.   Ex.
Above average.   A.A.   : Pilot Proficient
Average plus.   A+
Average.   A.   : Special
Below Average   B.A.   : Qualifications

REMARKS.

Date :- 19·1·45

CHIEF FLYING INSTRUCTOR

19 JAN 1945

O.C. TRAINING WING, NO. 73, O.T.U. R.A.F.

							17.			
199·00	205·30	21·10	18·00	1·10				41·55	53·40	5·00	59·45
(1)	(2)	(3)	(4)	(5)	(6)	(7)	(8)	(9)	(10)	(11)	(12)	(13)	(14)

YEAR 1945		AIRCRAFT		PILOT, OR 1ST PILOT	2ND PILOT, PUPIL OR PASSENGER	DUTY (INCLUDING RESULTS AND REMARKS)
MONTH	DATE	Type	No.			
		—	—	—	—	TOTALS BROUGHT FORWARD
						8. R. F. U
APRIL	3.	HARVARD		W/O GODFREY	SELF	DUAL CHECK.
"	3	THUNDERBOLT		SELF	—	FAMILIARISATION & RECCE.
"	5.	THUNDERBOLT	FL.731.	SELF.	—	FLIGHT. FORMATION.
"	10.	THUNDERBOLT	FL.774	SELF.	—	DIVE BOMBING.
"	10.	THUNDERBOLT	FL.774	SELF	—	CROSS COUNTRY.
"	12	THUNDERBOLT	KL.284	SELF.	—	DIVE BOMBING.
"	12	THUNDERBOLT	KL.284	SELF.	—	DIVE BOMBING.
"	12.	HARVARD.	FE.786.	P/O. PYEMAN	SELF	I.F.
"	14.	THUNDERBOLT	KL.176.	SELF.	—	FORMATION.
"	17.	THUNDERBOLT	KL.254	SELF.	—	FORMATION OXYGEN CLIMB.
"	19.	THUNDERBOLT	FL.731.	SELF.	"	LOW FLYING & AEROBATICS.
"	19.	THUNDERBOLT	HD.207	SELF.	"	AIR TO AIR CINE.
"	22.	THUNDERBOLT	FL.774	SELF.	—	AIR TO AIR ATTACKS.
"	25.	THUNDERBOLT	KL.838	SELF.	—	CINE' EXERCISE.
"	25	THUNDERBOLT.	KL.284	SELF.	—	SQUADRON FORMATION.
"	26.	THUNDERBOLT	KL.274.	SELF.	—	N/F TEST.
"	26	THUNDERBOLT	KL.274	SELF	—	LOCAL N/F.
"	26.	THUNDERBOLT	KL.274	SELF	—	LOCAL N/F.
"	30.	THUNDERBOLT.	KL.286	SELF.	—	SQUADRON FORMATION.
MAY	1.	THUNDERBOLT	FL.796	SELF.	—	LOW FLYING & AEROBATICS.
"	1.	THUNDERBOLT	KL.226	SELF.	—	SQUADRON HEIGHT CLIMB.
"	1.	THUNDERBOLT	KL.226	SELF.	—	CINE' EXERCISE.
"	3.	THUNDERBOLT	FL.774	SELF.	—	A.-G.

GRAND TOTAL [Cols. (1) to (10)]
.... Hrs. .... Mins.   TOTALS CARRIED FORWARD

Appendix V   151

Single-Engine Aircraft				Multi-Engine Aircraft						Passenger	Instr/Cloud Flying (Incl. in cols. (1) to (10))		Link Trainer
Day		Night		Day			Night					Dual	Pilot	
Dual	Pilot	Dual	Pilot	Dual	1st Pilot	2nd Pilot	Dual	1st Pilot	2nd Pilot				
(1)	(2)	(3)	(4)	(5)	(6)	(7)	(8)	(9)	(10)	(11)	(12)	(13)	(14)
199.00	205.30	21.10	18.00	1.10						41.55	53.40	5.00	64.45
	YELLAHANKA			INDIA									
.40													
	1.20												
	1.10												1.00
	1.10												
	2.15										1.00		
	.50												
	.50												
1.00											1.00		
	1.00												1.00
	1.15												
	1.30												
	1.10												
	1.30												
	.50												.40
	1.40												
	1.00			SUMMARY FOR APRIL 1945			HARVARD .. 1.40						
	1	1.00		UNIT: 8 R.F.U.			THUNDERBOLT .. 14.7 19.30						
			1.00	SIGNED .... s/Ldr O.C. 8.R.F.U.								NIGHT. 2.00		
	2.00			R. Taylor.										
	1.30												
	1.05			SIGNED ..R.W.Wilson.... O.C. FLIGHT.										
	.55												
	.50												
200.40	228.50	21.10	20.00							41.55	54.40	8.00	67.25
(1)	(2)	(3)	(4)	(5)	(6)	(7)	(8)	(9)	(10)	(11)	(12)	(13)	(14)

YEAR 1943		AIRCRAFT		PILOT, OR 1ST PILOT	2ND PILOT, PUPIL OR PASSENGER	DUTY (INCLUDING RESULTS AND REMARKS)
MONTH	DATE	Type	No.			TOTALS BROUGHT FORWARD
MAY	3.	THUNDERBOLT	KL.176	SELF	—	17 - G.
,,	4.	THUNDERBOLT	KL.233	SELF	—	SQDRN. DIVE BOMBING & LOW LEVEL DISPLAY
				SUMMARY FOR:	8. R.F.U.	THUNDERBOLT.
				UNIT:	8. R.F.U.	
				DATE:	5:5:45	HARVARD.
				SIGNATURE:	A. Findon	

GRAND TOTAL [Cols. (1) to (10)]
473 Hrs. ... Mins.   TOTALS CARRIED FORWARD

SINGLE-ENGINE AIRCRAFT				MULTI-ENGINE AIRCRAFT							PASS-ENGER	INSTR/CLOUD FLYING [incl. in cols. (1) to (10)]		LINK TRAINER
DAY		NIGHT		DAY			NIGHT						
DUAL	PILOT	DUAL	PILOT	DUAL	1ST PILOT	2ND PILOT	DUAL	1ST PILOT	2ND PILOT		DUAL	PILOT	
(1)	(2)	(3)	(4)	(5)	(6)	(7)	(8)	(9)	(10)	(11)	(12)	(13)	(14)
200·40	228·50	21·10	20·00							41·55	54·40	6·00	67·25
	·50												
	1·30												
—	26·10	—	2·00										—
				E.F. Johnson S/L O.C 8.R.F.U										2·40
1·40	—	—	—	R. Wilson F/O. O.C FLT							1·00		

34 Squadron

Year 1945		Aircraft		Pilot, or 1st Pilot	2nd Pilot, Pupil or Passenger	Duty (Including Results and Remarks)
Month	Date	Type	No.			Totals Brought Forward
June						
"	19	Thunderbolt	C.14	Self	—	Recce, Formation & Practice Strafe
"	19	Thunderbolt	L.25	Self	—	Practice Flying, Formation
"	20	Thunderbolt	F	Self	—	Formation & General Flying
"	20	Thunderbolt	F	Self	—	Aircraft Search
"	23	Thunderbolt	Y	Self	—	Practice Ops
"	25	Thunderbolt	H	Self	—	Strafe Village. Toungoo Area
"	27	Thunderbolt	H	Self	—	Strafe Troops in Road Camps

Summary for June 1945
Unit: 34 Squadron
Date: 31:6:45
Signature: J. Lindon

Thunderbolt.
Ops. Hours.
Non-Ops Hours.

July	5	Thunderbolt	C	Self	—	Bomb & Strafe Gun Pos. E of Mohpalin
"	6	Thunderbolt	F	Self	—	Bomb and Strafe W. of Moh...
"	9	Thunderbolt	A	Self	—	Bomb & Strafe Troops S.W. Toungoo
"	11	Thunderbolt	W	Self	—	A & E Test
"	11	Thunderbolt	F	Self	—	A & E Test
"	17	Thunderbolt	F	Self	—	Bomb & Strafe Mawchi Road
"	20	Thunderbolt	F	Self	—	Bomb & Strafe Village Pyu Area
"	21	Thunderbolt	F	Self	—	Toungoo to Base
"	23	Thunderbolt	F	Self	—	Air & Consumption Test
"	24	Thunderbolt	F	Self	—	Bomb & Strafe Village Pyu Area

Grand Total [Cols. (1) to (10)]
501 Hrs. 15 Mins.   Totals Carried Forward

Appendix V 155

SINGLE-ENGINE AIRCRAFT		MULTI-ENGINE AIRCRAFT						PASS-ENGER	INSTR/CLOUD FLYING (Incl. in cols. (1) to (10))		LINK TRAINER
DAY		NIGHT		DAY			NIGHT				
DUAL	PILOT	DUAL	PILOT	DUAL	1ST PILOT	2ND PILOT	DUAL	1ST PILOT	2ND PILOT		DUAL	PILOT	
(1)	(2)	(3)	(4)	(5)	(6)	(7)	(8)	(9)	(10)	(11)	(12)	(13)	(14)

BURMA.

KINMAGON – MEIKTILA

	200·40	231:	21·10	20·00							64·55	54·40	6·00	67·25
		1·15												
		1·10												
		1·10												
		3·10			NOT FOUND.									
		1·05												
		·40			RECALLED DUE TO BAD WEATHER							·20		
		1·30			FORCED TO RETURN BY LOW CLOUD							·40		
		3·30												
		2·10			J.K.Williamson F/Lt O.C. FLIGHT.									
		7·50			R.A.Douglas S/Ldr O.C. Sqdn.									

		3·30			JOB DONE.									
		2·45			ABORTIVE. VERY DIRTY WEATHER. LOST ONE							1·00		
		1·50			ABORTIVE. MORE DICEY WEATHER. LOST ONE							·40		
		·25												
		·15												
		2·10			TARGET AREA WELL PRANGED									
		3·10			VILLAGE BLASTED. BLASTED WEATHER. LAND TOUNGOU. En						1·00			
		·55			D.W. WENT IN ON T/O.									
		·40												
		2·30			GOOD TRIP RESULTS at									
	200·40	259·15	21·10	20·00							64·55	54·40	9·40	67·25

YEAR 1945		AIRCRAFT		PILOT, OR 1ST PILOT	2ND PILOT, PUPIL OR PASSENGER	DUTY (INCLUDING RESULTS AND REMARKS)
MONTH	DATE	Type	No.			
—	—	—	—	—	—	TOTALS BROUGHT FORWARD
July	28	Thunderbolt	KJ201 F	Self	—	Bomb & Strafe Village, Pyu...
"	30	Thunderbolt	F	Self	—	Bomb & Strafe Village Upper S...
"	30	Thunderbolt	F	Self	—	Bomb & Strafe Mytkio Area Vill...
"	31	Thunderbolt	C	Self	—	A&E Test
				F/Lt. OC BFlt	SUMMARY FOR: UNIT: DATE: SIGNATURE	July 1945 — Thunderbolt I 34 Squadron — OPS Hours 31:7:45 — NON-OPS Hours A. Lindon
Aug	3	Thunderbolt	C	Self	—	Bomb & Strafe N. of Naungashe
"	4	Thunderbolt	C	Self	—	Bomb Jap Dug In Pos. Strafe Tsasha...
"	6	Thunderbolt	A	Self	—	Weather Recce
"	6	Thunderbolt	F	Self	—	A.E. and Power Check
"	12	Thunderbolt	F	Self	—	Bomb & Strafe Ferry Pt. Lower Si...
"	14	Thunderbolt	O.K.	Self	—	Weather Recce
"	18	Thunderbolt	F	Self	—	Meiktila to Zaymtkwan
"	28	Thunderbolt	R	Self	—	Leaflet Drop
"	29	Thunderbolt	E	Self	—	Leaflet Drop. Kra Tjuri
"	29	Thunderbolt	A	Self	—	Leaflet Drop. Thabyuzayiat
				F/Lt. OC...	SUMMARY FOR: UNIT: DATE: SIGNATURE	August — Thunderbolt I 34 Squadron — OPS Hours 31:8:45 — NON-OPS Hours A. Lindon

GRAND TOTAL [Cols. (1) to (10)] 530 Hrs. 10 Mins. TOTALS CARRIED FORWARD

Appendix V   157

SINGLE-ENGINE A... DAY										INSTR/CLOUD FLYING [Incl. in cols. (1) to (10)]		LINK TRAINER
DUAL (1)	PILOT (2)	D...								DUAL (12)	PILOT (13)	(14)
200·40	259·15	21·...								4·40	9·40	67·25
	3·00											
	2·50										1·40	
	3·20											
	·40											
	25·5									1 LT. 04 SQUADRON		
	2·15											
											11·55 /45	
											1·00	
											·50	
											1·55	
											C PRANGED 1·00	
											NO DROP	
	1·00											
	1·55		VERY SUCCESSFUL								·20	
	16·30		OPS. HOURS							J.L. Williamson	F/LT O.C. Sqdn	
	2·45		PROGRESSIVE 4345 TOTAL									
200·40	288·20	21·10	20·00							64·55	54·40	67·25
(1)	(2)	(3)	(4)	(5)	(6)	(7)	(8)	(9)	(10)	(11)	(12)(13)	(14)

LEAFLET TELLS THE BURMESE THAT THE WAR HAD ENDED

YEAR 1945		AIRCRAFT		PILOT, OR 1ST PILOT	2ND PILOT, PUPIL OR PASSENGER	DUTY (INCLUDING RESULTS AND REMARKS)
MONTH	DATE	Type	No.			TOTALS BROUGHT FORWARD
SEP	8	HARVARD	KL184	F/O GRANT	SELF	ZAYATKWIN TO MEIKTILA
"	15	THUNDERBOLT		SELF	—	ZAYATKWIN — MEIKTILA — RETURN
					SUMMARY FOR: SEPTEMBER	
				F/O O.C. B. FLT	UNIT: 42 SQUADRON THUNDERBOLT II	
					DATE: 1:9:45	
					SIGNATURE: A. Linden	
OCT	5	THUNDERBOLT	J	SELF	—	AIR TEST
"	9	THUNDERBOLT	L	SELF	—	TO ZAYATKWIN & RETURN
"	12	THUNDERBOLT	T	SELF	—	CROSS COUNTRY & AEROBATICS
"	15	THUNDERBOLT	T	SELF	—	SECTION QUARTER ATT'K
					SUMMARY FOR: OCTOBER	
					UNIT: 42 SQUADRON THUNDERBOLT II	
					DATE: 22:10:45	
					SIGNATURE: A. Linden	
OCT	25	DAKOTA	KL268	F/O —	SELF	MEIKTILA — CALCUTTA
NOV	14	DAKOTA	KL211	F/O —	SELF	CALCUTTA — MEIKTILA
"	16	THUNDERBOLT	KL225	SELF	—	MEIKTILA — PEGU, RETURN
"	21	THUNDERBOLT	KL221	SELF	—	TOUNGOO — PROME, MYNGYAN — DAS
"	26	THUNDERBOLT	KL235	SELF	—	MEIKTILA — PEGU — RETURN
					SUMMARY FOR: NOVEMBER	
					UNIT: 42 SQUADRON THUNDERBOLT II	
					SIGNATURE: A. Linden	

GRAND TOTAL [Cols. (1) to (10)] 547 Hrs 50 Mins.   TOTALS CARRIED FORWARD

Appendix V 159

SINGLE-ENGINE AIRCRAFT				MULTI-ENGINE AIRCRAFT						PASS-ENGER	INSTR/CLOUD FLYING [incl. in cols. (1) to (10)]		LINK TRAINER
DAY		NIGHT		DAY			NIGHT						
DUAL	PILOT	DUAL	PILOT	DUAL	1ST PILOT	2ND PILOT	DUAL	1ST PILOT	2ND PILOT		DUAL	PILOT	
(1)	(2)	(3)	(4)	(5)	(6)	(7)	(8)	(9)	(10)	(11)	(12)	(13)	(14)
200.40	288.20	21.10	20.00		42			SQUADRON		64.55	54.40	14.25	67.25
						MEIKTILA				2.00			
	2.45											1.10	
	2.45									2.00			
	.30												
	2.45											.40	
	2.15												
	1.30												
	7.00												
							S/L O.C. 42 SQDRN						
										3.00			
										3.00			
	2.15											.50	
	3.00											.10	
	2.40											.40	
	7.55						F/L O.C. 42 SQDRN						
200.40	306.00	21.10	20.00							72.00	54.40	17.35	67.25
(1)	(2)	(3)	(4)	(5)	(6)	(7)	(8)	(9)	(10)	(11)	(12)	(13)	(14)

YEAR 1945		AIRCRAFT		PILOT, OR 1ST PILOT	2ND PILOT, PUPIL OR PASSENGER	DUTY (INCLUDING RESULTS AND REMARKS)
MONTH	DATE	Type	No.			
						TOTALS BROUGHT FORWARD
SEP	8	HARVARD	KL184	P/O GRANT	SELF	ZAYATKWIN TO MEIKTILA
"	15	THUNDERBOLT		SELF	—	ZAYATKWIN – MEIKTILA – RETURN
					SUMMARY FOR:	SEPTEMBER
				G/O O.C. B. FLT	UNIT:	42 SQUADRON THUNDERBOLT II
					DATE:	1:9:45
					SIGNATURE:	A. Findon
OCT	5	THUNDERBOLT	J	SELF	—	AIR TEST
"	8	THUNDERBOLT	L	SELF	—	TO ZAYATKWIN & RETURN
"	12	THUNDERBOLT	T	SELF	—	CROSS COUNTRY & AEROBATICS
"	15	THUNDERBOLT	T	SELF	—	SECTION QUARTER ATTACKS
					SUMMARY FOR:	OCTOBER
					UNIT:	42 SQUADRON THUNDERBOLT II
					DATE:	22:10:45
					SIGNATURE:	A. Findon
OCT	25	DAKOTA	KL268	F/O —	SELF	MEIKTILA – CALCUTTA
NOV	14	DAKOTA	KL211	F/O —	SELF	CALCUTTA – MEIKTILA
"	16	THUNDERBOLT	KL225	SELF	—	MEIKTILA – PEGU, RETURN
"	21	THUNDERBOLT	KL221	SELF	—	TOUNGOO – PROME, MYNGYAN – TJASO
"	26	THUNDERBOLT	KL235	SELF	—	MEIKTILA – PEGU – RETURN
					SUMMARY FOR:	NOVEMBER
					UNIT:	42 SQUADRON THUNDERBOLT II
					SIGNATURE:	A. Findon

GRAND TOTAL [Cols. (1) to (10)] 547 Hrs. 50 Mins.   TOTALS CARRIED FORWARD

Appendix V   161

	SINGLE-ENGINE AIRCRAFT				MULTI-ENGINE AIRCRAFT						PASS-ENGER	INSTR/CLOUD FLYING (incl. in cols. (1) to (10))		LINK TRAINER
	DAY		NIGHT		DAY		NIGHT							
DUAL	PILOT	DUAL	PILOT	DUAL	1ST PILOT	2ND PILOT	DUAL	1ST PILOT	2ND PILOT		DUAL	PILOT	
(1)	(2)	(3)	(4)	(5)	(6)	(7)	(8)	(9)	(10)	(11)	(12)	(13)	(14)
200.40	288.20	21.10	20.00	42 SQUADRON						64.55	54.40	14.25	67.25
					MEIKTILA					2.00			
	2.45											1.10	
	2.45									2.00			
	.30												
	2.45											.40	
	2.15												
	1.30												
	7.00												
								S/L O.C. 42 SQDRN					
										3.00			
										3.00			
	2.15											.50	
	3.00											1.10	
	2.40											.40	
	7.55												
								F/Lt. O.C. 42 SQDRN					
200.40	306.00	21.10	20.00							72.00	54.40	17.35	67.25
(1)	(2)	(3)	(4)	(5)	(6)	(7)	(8)	(9)	(10)	(11)	(12)	(13)	(14)

YEAR 1946		AIRCRAFT		PILOT, OR 1ST PILOT	2ND PILOT, PUPIL OR PASSENGER	DUTY (INCLUDING RESULTS AND REMARKS)
MONTH	DATE	Type	No.			
						TOTALS BROUGHT FORWARD
						3. S.F.T.U.
Jan.	21	HARVARD	779	F/O MACDONALD	SELF	RECCE & AEROBATICS
"	22	HARVARD	901	F/S PYNE-GILBERT	SELF	RECCE & AEROBATICS
"	22	SPITFIRE VIII	993	SELF	—	RECCE & AEROBATICS
"	23	SPIT. VIII	222	SELF	—	RANGE EST. & AERO'S
"	24	HARVARD	901	F/O SHANKS	SELF	EX. D.2. CINE
"	24	SPIT. VIII	439	SELF	—	AEROBATICS
"	25	SPIT. VIII	617	SELF	—	EX. F.2 CINE
"	25	SPIT. VIII	993	SELF	—	TOW LINE
"	26	SPIT. VIII	993	SELF	—	EX. F.3. CINE
"	28	HARVARD	901	F/O SHANKS	SELF	EX. F.4
"	28	SPIT. VIII	993	SELF	—	EX. F.4 CINE
"	29	SPIT. VIII	222	SELF	—	SNAP CINE
"	30	SPIT. VIII	403	SELF	—	TACTICAL EXERCISE
"	31	SPIT. VIII	403	SELF	—	SNAP CINE & PRACTICE DIVES
					SUMMARY FOR: UNIT: DATE: SIGNATURE	JANUARY 3 F.S.T.U. HARVARD 31:1:46. SPITFIRE
FEB	1	SPIT VIII	439	SELF	—	TACTICAL EXERCISE
"	2	SPIT VIII	323	SELF	—	PIN POINTING
"	3	HARVARD	901	F/O SHANKS	SELF	ROLLING ATTACKS

GRAND TOTAL [Cols. (1) to (10)] 564 Hrs. 20 Mins.   TOTALS CARRIED FORWARD

Appendix V   163

SINGLE-ENGINE AIRCRAFT		MULTI-ENGINE AIRCRAFT						PASS-ENGER	INSTR/CLOUD FLYING (Incl. in cols. (1) to (10))		LINK TRAINER
DAY		NIGHT		DAY			NIGHT						
DUAL	PILOT	DUAL	PILOT	DUAL	1ST PILOT	2ND PILOT	DUAL	1ST PILOT	2ND PILOT		DUAL	PILOT	
(1)	(2)	(3)	(4)	(5)	(6)	(7)	(8)	(9)	(10)	(11)	(12)	(13)	(14)
200.40	306.00	21.10	20.00		BHOPAL					72.00	54.40	17.35	67.25
.30				GROUND LOOP	MEMO:- DON'T BRING A HARVARD IN AT 140 IN A CROSS WIND								
.55													
	.45												
	1.00												
1.05													
	.45												
	1.00												
	.45												
	1.00												
1.00													
	1.00												
	1.00												
	1.15												
	1.00												
3.30					R.E. Shanks F/L F/LT O.C. FLIGHT.								
	9.30												
	1.15												
	1.15												
1.00													
205.10	318.00	21.10	20.00							74.00	54.40	17.35	67.25
(1)	(2)	(3)	(4)	(5)	(6)	(7)	(8)	(9)	(10)	(11)	(12)	(13)	(14)

YEAR 1946		AIRCRAFT		PILOT, OR 1ST PILOT	2ND PILOT, PUPIL OR PASSENGER	DUTY (INCLUDING RESULTS AND REMARKS)	
MONTH	DATE	Type	No.			TOTALS BROUGHT FORWARD	
FEB.	5.	SPITFIRE	459	SELF	—	DIVE BOMBING.	
"	6.	SPIT VIII	439	SELF	—	DIVE BOMBING.	
"	7.	SPIT VIII	459	SELF	—	SKIP BOMBING.	
"	8.	SPIT VIII	437	SELF	—	SKIP BOMBING.	
"	9.	SPIT VIII	323	SELF	—	DIVE BOMBING.	
"	12.	SPIT VIII	323	SELF	—	SECTION DIVE BOMBING.	
"	13.	HARVARD	901	SELF	F/O. WOOD	TO AGRA.	
"	14.	HARVARD	901	SELF	F/O WOOD	AGRA TO BASE.	
"	15.	SPIT VIII	323	SELF	—	SKIP BOMBING.	
"	18.	SPIT VIII	574	SELF	—	DUMMY OP.	
"	19.	SPIT VIII	222	SELF	—	DUMMY OP.	
"	21.	SPIT VIII	516	SELF	—	SECTION DIVE BOMBING.	
"	22.	HARVARD	901	SELF	—	BHOPAL TO POONA. } AMMO RUN	
"	23.	HARVARD	901	SELF	—	POONA "SANTA CRUZ".	
"	23.	HARVARD	901	SELF	—	SANTA CRUZ - BARODA - BASE.	
"	25.	SPIT VIII	862	SELF	—	AIR TEST	
"	27.	SPIT VIII	323	SELF	—	FORMATION.	
"	28.	SPIT VIII	323	SELF	—	STRAFFING.	
				S/L O.C. 3.F.S.T.U.	SUMMARY FOR:- UNIT:- DATE:- SIGNATURE.	FEBRUARY. 3. F.S.T.U. 28.2.46. R. Findon	HARVARD SPITFIRE

GRAND TOTAL [Cols. (1) to (10)]
586 Hrs. 30 Mins.   TOTALS CARRIED FORWARD

Appendix V   165

SINGLE-ENGINE AIRCRAFT				MULTI-ENGINE AIRCRAFT							PASS-ENGER	INSTR/CLOUD FLYING [Incl. in cols. (1) to (10)]		LINK TRAINER
DAY		NIGHT		DAY			NIGHT							
DUAL	PILOT	DUAL	PILOT	DUAL	1ST PILOT	2ND PILOT	DUAL	1ST PILOT	2ND PILOT			DUAL	PILOT	
(1)	(2)	(3)	(4)	(5)	(6)	(7)	(8)	(9)	(10)		(11)	(12)	(13)	(14)
205.10	318.00	21.00	20.00								74.00	54.40	17.35	67.30
	1.00													
	1.00													
	.45													
	.30													
	.45													
	.45													
	1.45												.30	
	1.55												.50	
	.35													
	1.30													
	1.35													
	.55													
	3.00			R.I.N. MUTINY — BLOODLESS OP 🍎									.20	
	.35													
	3.15													
	.25													
	1.25													
	.40													
1.00	10.30			- - - - - - - - - - - - -								F/LT. O.C. FLT.		
	14.50													
205.10	340.10	21.00	20.00								74.00	54.40	19.15	67.30
(1)	(2)	(3)	(4)	(5)	(6)	(7)	(8)	(9)	(10)		(11)	(12)	(13)	(14)

YEAR 1946		AIRCRAFT		PILOT, OR 1ST PILOT	2ND PILOT, PUPIL OR PASSENGER	DUTY (INCLUDING RESULTS AND REMARKS)	
MONTH	DATE	Type	No.			TOTALS BROUGHT FORWARD	
MARCH	1.	SPITFIRE VIII	323	SELF	—	AIR TO GROUND FIRING	
"	1.	SPIT. VIII	437	SELF.	—	GYRO GUNSIGHT PRACTISE	
"	1.	SPIT. VIII	617	SELF.	—	AIR TO GROUND FIRING	
					5½ O.C. 3 FSTU	SUMMARY FOR:— 3. F.S.T.U.	
						UNIT:— 3. F.S.T.U.	HARVARD
						DATE:— 3:3:46.	SPITFIRE MK VIII
						SIGNATURE. A. Findon	
"	22.	SPIT. VIII	939.	SELF.	"	FORMATION & TAIL CHASE	

GRAND TOTAL [Cols. (1) to (10)]
581 Hrs. 40 Mins.   TOTALS CARRIED FORWARD

Appendix V 167

\multicolumn{4}{c	}{SINGLE-ENGINE AIRCRAFT}	\multicolumn{6}{c	}{MULTI-ENGINE AIRCRAFT}	PASS-	\multicolumn{2}{c	}{INSTR/CLOUD}	LINK
\multicolumn{2}{c	}{DAY}	\multicolumn{2}{c	}{NIGHT}	\multicolumn{3}{c	}{DAY}	\multicolumn{3}{c	}{NIGHT}	ENGER	\multicolumn{2}{c	}{FLYING [Incl. in cols. (1) to (10)]}	TRAINER
DUAL	PILOT	DUAL	PILOT	DUAL	1ST PILOT	2ND PILOT	DUAL	1ST PILOT	2ND PILOT		DUAL	PILOT	
(1)	(2)	(3)	(4)	(5)	(6)	(7)	(8)	(9)	(10)	(11)	(12)	(13)	(14)
205·10	340·40	21·10	20·00							74·00	54·40	19·15	67·30
	·50												
	·40												
	·40												
4·30	10·30												
	26·30												
	1·00												
205·10	343·20	21·10	20·00							74·00	54·40	19·15	67·30
(1)	(2)	(3)	(4)	(5)	(6)	(7)	(8)	(9)	(10)	(11)	(12)	(13)	(14)

Brian *[signature]* O.C. FLT.

Year 1946		Aircraft		Pilot, or 1st Pilot	2nd Pilot, Pupil or Passenger	Duty (Including Results and Remarks)	
Month	Date	Type	No.			Totals Brought Forward	
May							
"	7	SPITFIRE VIII	936	SELF	—	AEROBATICS AND TAIL CHASE	
"	13	MOSQUITO VI	...	S/L. ADDICOTT	SELF	LOCAL FLYING & HOMING	
"	14	SPITFIRE XIV	187	SELF	—	FIRST SOLO. LOCAL AND AEROBATICS	
"	23	SPITFIRE XIV	187	SELF	—	AIR TEST	
"	27	SPITFIRE XIV	187	SELF	—	LOCAL AND AEROBATICS	
					SUMMARY FOR: —	MAY	
		[signature]		O.C. No. 28 Sqdn	UNIT: —	28 SQUADRON	SPITFIRE VIII
					DATE: —	1.6.46.	SPITFIRE XIV
					SIGNATURE: —	A. Findon	MOSQUITO VI
JUNE	4	SPITFIRE XIV	187	SELF	—	FORMATION	
"	6	SPITFIRE XIV	926	SELF	—	FORMATION	
"	7	SPITFIRE XIV	926	SELF	—	FORMATION	
"	8	SPITFIRE XIV	926	SELF	—	V PARADE. FLY PAST. K.L.	
"	12	SPITFIRE XIV	880	SELF	—	K.L. TO SELETAR, SINGAPORE	
"	13	SPITFIRE XIV	926	SELF	—	KINGS BIRTHDAY — FLY PAST	
"	13	SPITFIRE XIV	926	SELF	—	SELETAR TO KUALA LAMPUR	
"	24	SPITFIRE XIV	174	SELF	—	KUALA LAMPUR — SELETAR	
"	27	SPITFIRE XIV	160	SELF	—	AEROBATICS	

GRAND TOTAL [Cols. (1) to (10)]
602 Hrs. 55 Mins.   Totals Carried Forward

Appendix V   169

\multicolumn{4}{c}{SINGLE-ENGINE AIRCRAFT}	\multicolumn{6}{c}{MULTI-ENGINE AIRCRAFT}	PASS-ENGER	\multicolumn{2}{c}{INSTR/CLOUD FLYING [incl. in cols. (1) to (10)]}	LINK TRAINER
\multicolumn{2}{c}{DAY}	\multicolumn{2}{c}{NIGHT}	\multicolumn{3}{c}{DAY}	\multicolumn{3}{c}{NIGHT}				
DUAL	PILOT	DUAL	PILOT	DUAL	1ST PILOT	2ND PILOT	DUAL	1ST PILOT	2ND PILOT		DUAL	PILOT	
(1)	(2)	(3)	(4)	(5)	(6)	(7)	(8)	(9)	(10)	(11)	(12)	(13)	(14)
202.10	343.20	21.10	20.00							74	54.30	19.15	67.30
				\multicolumn{6}{l}{28 SQUADRON — KUALA LAMPUR MALAYA}				
	1.00												
1.00													
	.20												
	.40												
	.40												
	1.00												
	1.40												
1.00													
	1.00												
	1.15												
	1.00												
	1.00												
	.45											.20	
	1.00												
	.45											.15	
	1.00											.20	
	.50												
206.10	355.35	21.10	20.00							74	54.30	20.10	67.30
(1)	(2)	(3)	(4)	(5)	(6)	(7)	(8)	(9)	(10)	(11)	(12)	(13)	(14)

YEAR 1946		AIRCRAFT		PILOT, OR 1ST PILOT	2ND PILOT, PUPIL OR PASSENGER	DUTY (INCLUDING RESULTS AND REMARKS)
MONTH	DATE	Type	No.			TOTALS BROUGHT FORWARD
						SUMMARY FOR: JUNE
				Smith F/O O.C. B FLT.		UNIT: 28 SQUADRON. SPITFIRE XIV
						DATE: 1:7:46
						SIGNATURE: A. Tudor
JULY.	1.	SPITFIRE XIV	286	SELF	—	FORMATION.
"	3.	SPITFIRE XIV	286	SELF.		MILD TAIL CHASE
"	5.	SPITFIRE XIV	161	SELF.		AIR TEST & AEROBATICS.
"	5.	SPITFIRE XIV	189	SELF.		AIR TEST & AEROBATICS
"	6.	HARVARD. II	991	SELF.	MAJ. COOK	LOCAL STOOGE.
"	10.	SPITFIRE XIV	880	SELF.	—	AIR TEST.
"	12.	SPITFIRE XIV	926.	SELF.	—	FORMATION.
"	15.	SPITFIRE XIV	880	SELF.	—	PHOTO RECCE.
"	16	SPITFIRE XIV	926	SELF	—	FORMATION.
"	17.	HARVARD.	991	SELF	SGT. BOUNCE.	I.F.
"	18.	SPITFIRE XIV	880	SELF	—	FORMATION.
"	19	SPITFIRE XIV	926	SELF.	—	ARMY CO-OP JOB.
"	22	SPITFIRE XIV	920	SELF	—	FORMATION.
"	23.	SPITFIRE XIV	926	SELF.	—	FORMATION.
"	25.	SPITFIRE XIV	926	SELF.	—	FORMATION & TAIL CHASE.

GRAND TOTAL [Cols. (1) to (10)]
618 Hrs 10 Mins.

TOTALS CARRIED FORWARD

Appendix V   171

YEAR 1952		AIRCRAFT		PILOT, OR 1ST PILOT	2ND PILOT, PUPIL OR PASSENGER	DUTY (INCLUDING RESULTS AND REMARKS)	
MONTH	DATE	Type	No.			TOTALS BROUGHT FORWARD	
				SUMMARY FOR :- JULY.			
				SUMMARY FOR :- 28 SQUADRON.	28.40	SPITFIRE XIV	
				UNIT :-	28 SQUADRON.		HARVARD
				DATE :-	1:8:46.		
				SIGNATURE :- A. Findon.			
						R.A.F. SOUTH CERNEY 2.F.T.S	
1952.							
MARCH	27.	HARVARD	OF.	F/Sgt. ORAM.	SELF	1-13.17.18.	
"	28.	HARVARD	OF.	F/Sgt. ORAM.	SELF	14	
"	31.	HARVARD	01.	F/Sgt. ORAM.	SELF	11-12.	
"	31.	HARVARD	01.	SELF.	—	13.	
				SUMMARY FOR MARCH 1952		HARVARD II B.	
				F/LT UNIT. R.A.F. SOUTH CERNEY.			
		OC "J" FLIGHT		DATE: MARCH 31 1952.			
		OC. No. 5 SQUADRON		S/LDR. SIGNATURE A.F. P/O			
APRIL	1.	HARVARD	OP.	F/Sgt. ORAM.	SELF	8, 9, 10, 14, 16, 17	
"	1	HARVARD	OP.	SELF	—	8, 9, 10, 17, 18.	
"	3.	HARVARD	OF.	SELF.	—	14. 11. 12. 18.	

GRAND TOTAL [Cols. (1) to (10)]
626 Hrs. 35 Mins.   TOTALS CARRIED FORWARD

Appendix V   173

I hereby certify that I understand the fuel, oil, hydraulic and pneumatic systems, also the emergency operations of the ..HARVARD. aircraft. I have received instructions and understand action to be taken in the event of fire and abandoning aircraft.

Signature.. *a. ...* F/o.

Date. 5.–5.–52 .... Instructor's Signature. .... Flgr

2·00									20	·20			
·30									10	·10			
1·00													
1·00	1·00												
3·30	1·00								·30				
2·20									·10				
	1·00												
	·45											·45	
212·0	373·35	21·00	20·00						74·00	56·00	21·10	68·25	
(1)	(2)	(3)	(4)	(5)	(6)	(7)	(8)	(9)	(10)	(11)	(12)	(13)	(14)

YEAR 1952		Aircraft		Pilot, or 1st Pilot	2nd Pilot, Pupil or Passenger	DUTY (Including Results and Remarks)
Month	Date	Type	No.			
—	—	—	—	—	—	Totals Brought Forward
APRIL	4	HARVARD	05	F/Sgt. ORAM	SELF	15 - 16
"	4	HARVARD	05	SELF	—	14 - 17 - 18
"	5	HARVARD	05	SELF	—	14 - 17
"	5	HARVARD	06	SELF	—	17
"	7	HARVARD	09	F/Sgt ORAM	SELF	17
"	7	HARVARD	05	SELF	—	11 - 12 - 17
"	7	HARVARD	01	F/Sgt. ORAM	SELF	19
"	7	HARVARD	01	SELF	—	19
"	9	HARVARD	OP	F/Sgt. ORAM	SELF	15
"	9	HARVARD	05	SELF	—	
"	9	HARVARD	05	SELF	—	
"	17	HARVARD	01	F/Sgt. ORAM	SELF	15
"	17	HARVARD	01	SELF	—	15
"	17	HARVARD	01	SELF	—	15
"	18	HARVARD	01	F/Sgt. ORAM	SELF	15
"	18	HARVARD	01	SELF	—	15
"	18	HARVARD	01	SELF	—	18
"	22	HARVARD	05	SELF	—	18
"	22	HARVARD	06	SELF	—	18
"	23	HARVARD	06	F/Sgt ORAM	SELF	15
"	24	HARVARD	06	SELF	—	15 - 18
"	25	HARVARD	05	SELF	—	15
"	28	HARVARD	04	F/Sgt ORAM	SELF	15

GRAND TOTAL [Cols. (1) to (10)]
650 Hrs. 20 Mins.   Totals Carried Forward

Appendix V 175

D GLASTRA.

Single-Engine Aircraft				Multi-Engine Aircraft						Pass-enger	Instr/Cloud Flying (Incl. in cols. (1) to (10))		Link Trainer
Day		Night		Day			Night						
Dual	Pilot	Dual	Pilot	Dual	1st Pilot	2nd Pilot	Dual	1st Pilot	2nd Pilot		Dual	Pilot	
(1)	(2)	(3)	(4)	(5)	(6)	(7)	(8)	(9)	(10)	(11)	(12)	(13)	(14)
212.0	373.35	21.00	20.00							74.00	56.00	21.10	68.25
1.00											.20		
	1.15												
	1.00												
	55												
	1.00												
.40												.20	
	55												
		1.00											
			1.00										
1.05											.40		
	1.00												
	1.00											.45	
1.10											40		
	1.00												
	1.05										.45		
1.15											.50		
	1.15										1.00		
	1.00												
	1.00												
	1.00												
1.00											.20	.10	
	1.00												
	1.00												
1.05												.40	1.00
219.15	388.05	22.00	21.00							74.00	61.20	22.20	69.25
(1)	(2)	(3)	(4)	(5)	(6)	(7)	(8)	(9)	(10)	(11)	(12)	(13)	(14)

Year 1952		Aircraft		Pilot, or 1st Pilot	2nd Pilot, Pupil or Passenger	Duty (Including Results and Remarks)
Month	Date	Type	No.			
						Totals Brought Forward
April	28	Harvard	OY	Self	—	15.
"	29	Harvard	OV	F/Sgt. Oram	Self.	
"	29	Harvard	OY	Self	—	15.
"	30	Harvard	OT.	Self.		15
				Summary for April 1952		Harvard II B
				Unit. R.A.F. South Cerney.		
				Date 30th April 1952		
				Signature:		
May	1.	Harvard.	OI.	Self.	—	15
"	1.	Harvard.	OP.	Self.	—	15
"	5	Harvard.	OH.	Self.	—	15
"	5	Harvard.	OP.	F/Sgt. Oram	Self	15
"	6	Harvard	OP	F/Sgt Oram	Self.	15 - S.B.A.
"	6	Harvard	OJ	Self	—	15 - S.B.A.
"	6	Harvard.	OJ.	Self.	—	15.
"	8.	Harvard	OJ	Self	—	15
"	8	Harvard	OJ	Self	—	15.
"	8	Harvard	OY	F/Sgt Rogers	Self	15. S.B.A.
"	9	Harvard	OH	Self	—	15.
"	12	Harvard	OJ.	Self	—	15 - 12 - 18

Grand Total [Cols. (1) to (10)]
667 Hrs. 10 Mins.   Totals Carried Forward

Appendix V 177

SINGLE-ENGINE AIRCRAFT				MULTI-ENGINE AIRCRAFT								PASS-ENGER	INSTR/CLOUD FLYING (incl. in cols. (1) to (10))		LINK TRAINER
DAY		NIGHT		DAY			NIGHT						
DUAL	PILOT	DUAL	PILOT	DUAL	1ST PILOT	2ND PILOT	DUAL	1ST PILOT	2ND PILOT		DUAL	PILOT	
(1)	(2)	(3)	(4)	(5)	(6)	(7)	(8)	(9)	(10)	(11)	(12)	(13)	(14)
219.15	388.0	22.00	21.00							74.00	61.20	22.20	69.25
	1.15										.35	.25	
1.30											.40		
	1.15										1.00		
	1.15										.50		
10.35	19.55	1.00	1.00								8.25	1.45	1.45
											CHECKED BY		
	.50												
	1.05										.45	.15	
	1.10										.55		
1.00											.20	.20	
1.00											.30	.10	
	1.00										.40	.10	
	1.00												
	1.00												
	1.00										.40	.10	
1.00											.40	-	
	1.30										1.10	.10	
	.25												
223.15	400.55	22.00	21.00							74.00	70.05	24.00	69.25
(1)	(2)	(3)	(4)	(5)	(6)	(7)	(8)	(9)	(10)	(11)	(12)	(13)	(14)

YEAR 1952		AIRCRAFT		PILOT, OR 1ST PILOT	2ND PILOT, PUPIL OR PASSENGER	DUTY (INCLUDING RESULTS AND REMARKS)
MONTH	DATE	Type	No.			
						TOTALS BROUGHT FORWARD
May	14	HARVARD	OF	SELF	—	15 - S.B.A
"	14	HARVARD	OJ	F/LT. BLUNDY	SELF.	I.R.T.
"	15	HARVARD	OJ	F/SGT. ORAM	SELF	15
"	15	HARVARD	OJ	F/LT. BUNDY	SELF.	I.R.T. (CONT.)
"	16	HARVARD	OF.	F/SGT. ORAM	SELF.	15 - S.B.A.
"	16	HARVARD	OF	F/LT. BLUNDY	SELF.	I.R.T.
"	19	HARVARD	OE.	F/O LIVERSIDGE	SELF.	F.H.T. 16-17-18.
"	19	HARVARD	OJ.	SELF.	—	15.
"	20	HARVARD	OE.	S/LDR HONEYMAN	SELF.	7,8,9,10,11,12,15,16,17,18

SUMMARY FOR MAY 1952 — HARVARD IIB.
UNIT R.A.F. SOUTH CERNEY
DATE: 20TH MAY 1952
SIGNATURE

SUMMARY FOR 23 REFRESHER — HARVARD IIB.
UNIT R.A.F. SOUTH CERNEY
DATE: 20TH MAY 1952
SIGNATURE

GRAND TOTAL [Cols. (1) to (10)] 678 Hrs 55 Mins. TOTALS CARRIED FORWARD

Appendix V 179

SINGLE-ENGINE AIRCRAFT				MULTI-ENGINE AIRCRAFT						PASS-ENGER	INSTR/CLOUD FLYING [Incl. in cols. (1) to (10)]		LINK TRAINER
DAY		NIGHT		DAY			NIGHT						
DUAL	PILOT	DUAL	PILOT	DUAL	1ST PILOT	2ND PILOT	DUAL	1ST PILOT	2ND PILOT		DUAL	PILOT	
(1)	(2)	(3)	(4)	(5)	(6)	(7)	(8)	(9)	(10)	(11)	(12)	(13)	(14)
223.15	400.55	22.00	21.00							74.00	70.05	24.00	69.25
	.40										.20	.10	
1.15											8.40	.30	
.40												.20	
1.00											.35	.20	
1.05											.40		
.50											.45		
1.00													
	1.10												
1.05												.05	
09.55	11.00										8.40	2.35	
				CHECKED BY:— Douglas Bruce /krs									
20.30	30.55	1.00	1.00								17.05	4.20	
				CHECKED BY:— Douglas Bruce /krs									
223.10	402.45	22.00	21.00							74.00	73.5	25.25	69.25
(1)	(2)	(3)	(4)	(5)	(6)	(7)	(8)	(9)	(10)	(11)	(12)	(13)	(14)

Year 1952		Aircraft		Pilot, or 1st Pilot	2nd Pilot, Pupil or Passenger	Duty (Including Results and Remarks)
Month	Date	Type	No.			Totals Brought Forward
June						
	7	Prentice	KV	F/Lt. Palmer	Self	CENTRAL FLYING SCHOOL
	7	Prentice	KV	F/Lt. Palmer	Self	1 - 22
	7	Prentice	KV	Self	Solo	13
	10	Prentice	KJ	Self	Solo	Familiarisation
	10	Prentice	KJ	F/Lt. Palmer	Self	4 · 11 · 12
	11	Prentice	KP	F/Lt. Palmer	Self	11 - 12
	11	Prentice	KP	Self	Solo	4 - 11 - 12
	12	Prentice	KP	Self	Solo	4 - 11 - 12
	12	Prentice	KP	F/Lt. Palmer	Self	
	12	Prentice	KP	Self	Solo	7 - 11 - 12
	14	Prentice	KP	Self	Solo	6 - 11 - 12 - 18
	16	Prentice	KP	F/Lt. Palmer	Self	No. 7 X Country
	16	Prentice	KU	Self	Solo	5 · 6, 11, 12
	16	Prentice	KP	Self	Solo	19
	16	Prentice	KP	F/Lt. Palmer	Self	19
	19	Prentice	KP	Self	Solo	Nav. 12
	19	Prentice	KP	F/Lt. Palmer	Self	7
	20	Prentice	KP	Self	Solo	11 - 12 - 6 - 7
	20	Prentice	KP	F/Lt. Palmer	Self	
	20	Prentice	KP	F/Lt. Palmer	Self	19
	20	Prentice		Self	Solo	Nav. & Precision
	20	Prentice		Self	Solo	

GRAND TOTAL [Cols. (1) to (10)]
702 Hrs. 30 Mins.   Totals Carried Forward

Appendix V 181

CENTRAL FLYING SCHOOL

Certified that I understand the Fuel and Oil systems, the Hydraulic system and its emergency operation; also the action in event of Fire and Abandoning by Parachute in the case of the following aircraft.

Certified also that I understand the starting, running up, running down, and stopping procedures of the engines as appropriate.

briefed on aircraft, ions.

.... fficer)

Init- ials.

	Signature	Instructors Signature
Harvard.	a. *illegible*	*illegible* M/O
Prentice.	a. *illegible*	C.R. Palmer Fw.o
Tiger Moth.		
VAMPIRE. Meteor.	a. *illegible*	*illegible* M/O
Chipmunk.		
Balliol.		

(1)	(2)	(3)	(4)	(5)	(6)	(7)	(8)	(9)	(10)	(11)	(12)	(13)	(14)
1·00													
	1·15												
1·00													
		1·15											
		1·20											
			1·15										
241·10	413·15	25·20	22·45							74·	73·40	25·25	70·25

YEAR 1952		AIRCRAFT		PILOT, OR 1ST PILOT	2ND PILOT, PUPIL OR PASSENGER	DUTY (INCLUDING RESULTS AND REMARKS)
MONTH	DATE	Type	No.	—	—	TOTALS BROUGHT FORWARD
JUNE	21	PRENTICE	KU	SELF	F/LT TOMKINS A.C. CARRILL	BASE – TANGMERE
"	22	PRENTICE	KU	SELF	" "	TANGMERE – BASE
"	23	PRENTICE	KP	F/LT PALMER	SELF	8.
"	23	PRENTICE	KP	SELF	SOLO	8.
"	24	PRENTICE	KP	SELF	SOLO	10 – 14
"	24	PRENTICE	KP	F/LT PALMER	SELF	10 – 14 – 18
"	25	PRENTICE	KK	F/LT HOWE	SELF	PROGRESS CHECK
"	25	PRENTICE	KP	SELF	SOLO	4
"	26	PRENTICE	KP	F/LT PALMER	SELF	9
"	26	PRENTICE	KP	SELF	SOLO	
"	27	PRENTICE	KP	F/LT PALMER	SELF	16 – 17
"	27	PRENTICE	KP	SELF	SOLO	16 – 17
"	30	PRENTICE	KL	SELF	SOLO	14 – 16 – 18

SUMMARY FOR JUNE 1952.
UNIT: – CENTRAL FLYING SCHOOL, S. CERNEY.
DATE: JUNE 30TH. 1952.
SIGNATURE

AIRCRAFT TYPES: PRENTICE
OTHER FLYING: –

July	1.	PRENTICE	KP	F/LT PALMER	SELF	9 – 17 – 11 – 12 .
"	1.	PRENTICE	KP	SELF	SOLO	14 – 18
"	3	PRENTICE	KV	F/LT PALMER	SELF	14.
"	3	PRENTICE	KL	SELF	SOLO	14.

GRAND TOTAL [Cols. (1) to (10)]
722 Hrs. 15 Mins.

TOTALS CARRIED FORWARD

Appendix V 183

SINGLE-ENGINE AIRCRAFT				MULTI-ENGINE AIRCRAFT						PASS-ENGER	INSTR/CLOUD FLYING [Incl. in cols. (1) to (10)]		LINK TRAINER
DAY		NIGHT		DAY			NIGHT						
DUAL	PILOT	DUAL	PILOT	DUAL	1ST PILOT	2ND PILOT	DUAL	1ST PILOT	2ND PILOT		DUAL	PILOT	
(1)	(2)	(3)	(4)	(5)	(6)	(7)	(8)	(9)	(10)	(11)	(12)	(13)	(14)
241·10	413·15	25·20	22·45							74	73·40	25·25	70·25
	·55												
	1·10											·15	
1·00													1·
	1·15												
	1·15												1·
1·05													
·50													1·
	1·10												
1·20													
	1·15												
1·00													1·
	1·15												
	1·15												
13·15	17·55	3·20	1·45		Chicken Ox					·35	25·40		4.
	2·5										LINK 4 hrs		
1·20													
	1·25												
1·00													
	1·15												
248·45	425·25	25·20	22·45							·74	73·40	25·40	74·25
(1)	(2)	(3)	(4)	(5)	(6)	(7)	(8)	(9)	(10)	(11)	(12)	(13)	(14)

Year 1952		Aircraft		Pilot, or 1st Pilot	2nd Pilot, Pupil or Passenger	Duty (Including Results and Remarks)
Month	Date	Type	No.			Totals Brought Forward
July	4	Prentice	KV	Self	Solo	4, 5, 6, 7, 11, 12, 15.
"	7	Prentice	KH.	Self	Solo	4, 5, 6, 7, 8, 9, 12, 18.
"	7	Prentice	KL.	Self	Solo.	9 - 12 - 18.
"	8	Prentice	KJ	Self.	Solo.	18.
				Continuation:		Central Flying School —
"	22	Harvard	NK	F/Lt. Ziesler.	Self	8, 10, 17, 18.
"	22	Harvard	NK	F/Lt. Ziesler.	Self	11, 12.
"	22	Harvard.	NK	Self.	Solo.	11, 12.
"	23	Harvard.	NZ.	F/Lt. Ziesler.	Self.	8, 10, 11, 12, 16, 18.
"	23	Harvard.	NZ.	Self.	Solo	11, 12, 18.
"	23	Harvard	NZ.	Self.	Solo.	8, 10, 11, 12, 18.
"	24	Harvard	NW	F/Lt. Hicks.	Self	11, 12, 18, 17.
"	24	Harvard	NW.	Self.	Solo	8, 10, 11, 12, 16, 18.
"	28	Harvard	NW	F/Lt. Hicks	Self	5, 15, 17.
"	28	Harvard.	NW.	Self.	Solo	11, 12, 17, 18.
"	31	Harvard	NW	F/Lt. Hicks	Self.	11, 12, 15, 18.
"	31	Harvard	NK.	Self.	Solo.	11, 12, 15, 17, 18.

Summary for July 1952
Unit: C.F.S.
Date: August 1st.
Signature:

Aircraft Types:
1. Prentice
2. Harvard

GRAND TOTAL [Cols. (1) to (10)]
740 Hrs. 45 Mins.

Totals Carried Forward

Appendix V   185

SINGLE-ENGINE AIRCRAFT				MULTI-ENGINE AIRCRAFT						PASS-ENGER	INSTR/CLOUD FLYING (Incl. in cols. (1) to (10))		LINK TRAINER
DAY		NIGHT		DAY			NIGHT						
DUAL	PILOT	DUAL	PILOT	DUAL	1ST PILOT	2ND PILOT	DUAL	1ST PILOT	2ND PILOT		DUAL	PILOT	
(1)	(2)	(3)	(4)	(5)	(6)	(7)	(8)	(9)	(10)	(11)	(12)	(13)	(14)
248.45	425.25	25.20	22.45							74	73.40	25.40	74.25
	2.30										.30	.40	
	1.00												
	1.10												
	1.00												
	LITTLE RISSINGTON												
.40													
.30													
	.15												
1.25													
	1.05												
	1.00												
1.20													
	1.20												
1.20											.30		
	1.15												
1.25											.30	.10	
	1.30												
2.20	8.20										.30	.40	
6.40	6.25										1.00	.10	
255.10	437.30	25.20	22.45							74	75.10	27.30	74.25
(1)	(2)	(3)	(4)	(5)	(6)	(7)	(8)	(9)	(10)	(11)	(12)	(13)	(14)

Year 1953		Aircraft		Pilot, or 1st Pilot	2nd Pilot, Pupil or Passenger	Duty (Including Results and Remarks)
Month	Date	Type	No.			Totals Brought Forward
MARCH	4	CHIPMUNK	WK518	SELF	HYMERS	15 A.B.F. 9c. 17a 17a 18
	4	CHIPMUNK	WK518	SELF	F/Lt. TAYLOR	1.T. 15a 6.c.f.
	4	CHIPMUNK	WK563	W/CMM. PEVELER	SELF	TEST.
	5	CHIPMUNK	WK518	SELF	JONKLAAS	15 a.6. 11.12.17a. 9c.10.
	9	CHIPMUNK	WK518	SELF	HYMERS	8.9c 10 6.17 6.18.27.
	9	CHIPMUNK	WK560	SELF	DIXON	8.9c.106.176.18.27
	10	CHIPMUNK	WK612	SELF	JONKLAAS	8.9c.10.11.12a.17a.
	10	CHIPMUNK	WK518	SELF	BURNETT	NAV. A.6.
	11	CHIPMUNK	WP838	SELF	HYMERS	15 AB. 17a. 18. 9c.
	12	CHIPMUNK	WP863	SELF	F/Lt. DAWES	1.T. 15a.6.
	12	CHIPMUNK	WK563	SELF	FRITH	NAV. A.6.
	12	CHIPMUNK	WP838	SELF	JONKLASS	15 a 6.
	13	CHIPMUNK	WP838	SELF	JONKLAAS	15 A.B. 11a. 12.17a.
	13	CHIPMUNK	WP838	SELF	DIXON	8.9c.10.17a 18.11a12.
	13	CHIPMUNK	WK612	SELF	HYMERS	15 t.
	13	CHIPMUNK	WK612	SELF	DIXON	15 t.
	14	CHIPMUNK	WK518	SELF	FRITH	21.
	14	CHIPMUNK	WK518	SELF	BURNETT	21.
	17	CHIPMUNK	WK612	F/Lt. HERBERT	SELF	C.F.S. STANDARDISATION.
	17	CHIPMUNK	WK612	SELF	FRITH	9c. 11.12.17 B.18.
	18	CHIPMUNK	WK612	SELF	DIXON	15 A.B.F. g. c.A.
	18	CHIPMUNK	WK612	SELF	HARE	15 A.B.F. g. c. A.
	19	CHIPMUNK	WK612	SELF	FRITH	15 A.B.

GRAND TOTAL [Cols. (1) to (10)]
953 Hrs. 20 Mins.   TOTALS CARRIED FORWARD

Appendix V   187

METEOR

Meteor VII WG. 947 of No. 231 O.C.U., Royal Air Force Merryfield on 4th November, 1955 at 1356Z

Pilot: Plt. Off. M.L. Jonklaas
Total Solo 145 Solo Type 44

On take-off for first solo at the Unit the starboard engine lost power at about 50 feet. The aircraft yawed to starboard, rolled and dived in inverted from about 150 feet. The pilot was killed. The Court of Inquiry considered that, had the correct drill been carried out, i.e., throttle back the port engine to maintain directional and lateral control, at worst a landing in the clear area ahead wheels – up would have resulted. This accident ought not to have had fatal results. See Engines Section.

******** UNCLASSIFIED MAJOR FLYING ACCIDENT ********

RECORD OF SERVICE

UNIT	FROM	TO	UNIT	FROM	TO
A.C.R.C. LONDON	6:7:42	26:7:42	10 R.C.S. POONA	7:12:45	12:1:46
27 E.T.W. LUDLOW	27:7:42	24:8:42	3 S.F.T.U. BHOPAL	4:1:46	3:4:46
3 I.T.W. TORQUAY	24:8:42	14:1:43	28 SQUADRON. MALAYA	4:5:46	
9 E.F.T.S. Ansty	15:1:43	12:3:43	I.O.R.C. SINGAPORE	8:8:46	12:8:46
HEATON PARK. MANCHESTER	12:3:43	15:4:43	DEMOBILISED	7:9:46	25:3:52
31 Depot MONCTON	15:4:43	29:4:43	C.F.S. SOUTH CERNEY	25:3:52	15:7:52
31 E.F.T.S. DE WINTON	29:4:43	7:8:43	C.F.S. LITTLE RISSINGTON	15:7:52	5:9:52
34 S.F.T.S. MEDICINE HAT	8:8:43	26:11:43	R.A.F. COLLEGE, CRANWELL	15:9:52	
No.1. F.I.S. TRENTON ONT	11:12:43	11:2:44			
MONCTON 31. P.D	28:2:44	4:4:44			
R.A.F. HARROGATE	7:4:44	16:4:44			
R.A.F. WHITLEY BAY N.C.O School	20:5:44	21:6:44			
7 P.R.C. PADGATE	21:6:44	27:6:44			
7 E.F.T.S. DESFORD	27:6:44	2:6:44			
7 (P) A.F.U. PETERBORO	29:6:44	24:8:44			
22 P.T.C. MORECAMBE	14:9:44	28:8:44			
21. P.D.C. CAIRO	12:9:44	18:9:44			
73. O.T.U. FAYID	18:10:44	19:1:45			
8 (T) F.U BANGALORE	31:3:45	24:5:45			
P.D.C. KARACHI	12:2:45	19:2:45			
P.D.C. POONA	21:2:45	28:2:45			
JUNGLE SCHOOL	28:2:45	23:3:45			
(TRANSIT) CALCUTTA	28:5:45	4:6:45			
34 SQDRN. BURMA	6:6:45	7:9:45			
	7:9:45	25:11:45			

AIRCRAFT FLOWN

AIRCRAFT	ENGINE	AIRCRAFT	ENGINE	AIRCRAFT	ENGINE
D.H.82a Tiger Moth	Gipsy Mag. 130"/130"				
Fairchild Cornell I & II	Ranger 175hp				
Harvard I & IIb	Pratt &550hp Whitney Wasp				
Master II	Mercury 20 850hp				
Thunderbolt I & II	Pratt Whitney 2,000 H.P. Twin Wasp				
Spitfire VIII	Merlin 66				
Spitfire XIV	Griffin				
Prentice	Gypsy Queen				
Vampire	Goblin				
Chipmunk 10	Gypsy Major				
Meteor IV/VII	Derwent				